C-2872   CAREER EXAMINATION SERIES

This is your PASSBOOK for...

Highway Construction Inspector

*Test Preparation Study Guide
Questions & Answers*

COPYRIGHT NOTICE

This book is SOLELY intended for, is sold ONLY to, and its use is RESTRICTED to individual, bona fide applicants or candidates who qualify by virtue of having seriously filed applications for appropriate license, certificate, professional and/or promotional advancement, higher school matriculation, scholarship, or other legitimate requirements of education and/or governmental authorities.

This book is NOT intended for use, class instruction, tutoring, training, duplication, copying, reprinting, excerption, or adaptation, etc., by:

1) Other publishers
2) Proprietors and/or Instructors of "Coaching" and/or Preparatory Courses
3) Personnel and/or Training Divisions of commercial, industrial, and governmental organizations
4) Schools, colleges, or universities and/or their departments and staffs, including teachers and other personnel
5) Testing Agencies or Bureaus
6) Study groups which seek by the purchase of a single volume to copy and/or duplicate and/or adapt this material for use by the group as a whole without having purchased individual volumes for each of the members of the group
7) Et al.

Such persons would be in violation of appropriate Federal and State statutes.

PROVISION OF LICENSING AGREEMENTS – Recognized educational, commercial, industrial, and governmental institutions and organizations, and others legitimately engaged in educational pursuits, including training, testing, and measurement activities, may address request for a licensing agreement to the copyright owners, who will determine whether, and under what conditions, including fees and charges, the materials in this book may be used them. In other words, a licensing facility exists for the legitimate use of the material in this book on other than an individual basis. However, it is asseverated and affirmed here that the material in this book CANNOT be used without the receipt of the express permission of such a licensing agreement from the Publishers. Inquiries re licensing should be addressed to the company, attention rights and permissions department.

All rights reserved, including the right of reproduction in whole or in part, in any form or by any means, electronic or mechanical, including photocopying, recording, or by any information storage and retrieval system, without permission in writing from the Publisher.

Copyright © 2024 by
National Learning Corporation

212 Michael Drive, Syosset, NY 11791
(516) 921-8888 • www.passbooks.com
E-mail: info@passbooks.com

PUBLISHED IN THE UNITED STATES OF AMERICA

PASSBOOK® SERIES

THE *PASSBOOK® SERIES* has been created to prepare applicants and candidates for the ultimate academic battlefield – the examination room.

At some time in our lives, each and every one of us may be required to take an examination – for validation, matriculation, admission, qualification, registration, certification, or licensure.

Based on the assumption that every applicant or candidate has met the basic formal educational standards, has taken the required number of courses, and read the necessary texts, the *PASSBOOK® SERIES* furnishes the one special preparation which may assure passing with confidence, instead of failing with insecurity. Examination questions – together with answers – are furnished as the basic vehicle for study so that the mysteries of the examination and its compounding difficulties may be eliminated or diminished by a sure method.

This book is meant to help you pass your examination provided that you qualify and are serious in your objective.

The entire field is reviewed through the huge store of content information which is succinctly presented through a provocative and challenging approach – the question-and-answer method.

A climate of success is established by furnishing the correct answers at the end of each test.

You soon learn to recognize types of questions, forms of questions, and patterns of questioning. You may even begin to anticipate expected outcomes.

You perceive that many questions are repeated or adapted so that you can gain acute insights, which may enable you to score many sure points.

You learn how to confront new questions, or types of questions, and to attack them confidently and work out the correct answers.

You note objectives and emphases, and recognize pitfalls and dangers, so that you may make positive educational adjustments.

Moreover, you are kept fully informed in relation to new concepts, methods, practices, and directions in the field.

You discover that you are actually taking the examination all the time: you are preparing for the examination by "taking" an examination, not by reading extraneous and/or supererogatory textbooks.

In short, this PASSBOOK®, used directedly, should be an important factor in helping you to pass your test.

HIGHWAY CONSTRUCTION INSPECTOR

WHAT THE JOB INVOLVES:

Highways Construction Inspectors, under general supervision, perform technical work in the inspection of construction, repair and maintenance of roads, sewers and appurtenances, pavements and sidewalks. They inspect the grading, paving and repaving of streets; inspect the maintenance, repair and construction of sewers and appurtenances, house sewer connections, retaining walls, streets and street openings; inspect the construction and repair of water, sewer and utility manholes and street sidewalks; inspect private property; in testing laboratories for asphalt or concrete plants, check all materials used as to quality and grade; witness the making of concrete and other test cylinders; check the size of street openings and the satisfactory restoration of pavement or sidewalk; investigate complaints and reports on findings; maintain records and prepares comprehensive reports; keep daily records of the number and types of skilled and unskilled labor employed and mechanical equipment and material used; drive a passenger car or light truck to and from work assignments; may supervise and train subordinates.

THE TEST

The multiple-choice test may include questions on the construction, repair, a maintenance of highways, roads, pavements, sidewalks, sewers and proper safety and work practices; principles and practices of civil engineering; modern methods and techniques as applied to the construction and maintenance of highways; written expression, including the preparation of forms and reports; written comprehension; arithmetic and other job related calculations; recognition of potential problems and the development of logical solutions; supervision of subordinates; and other related areas.

HOW TO TAKE A TEST

I. YOU MUST PASS AN EXAMINATION

A. WHAT EVERY CANDIDATE SHOULD KNOW

Examination applicants often ask us for help in preparing for the written test. What can I study in advance? What kinds of questions will be asked? How will the test be given? How will the papers be graded?

As an applicant for a civil service examination, you may be wondering about some of these things. Our purpose here is to suggest effective methods of advance study and to describe civil service examinations.

Your chances for success on this examination can be increased if you know how to prepare. Those "pre-examination jitters" can be reduced if you know what to expect. You can even experience an adventure in good citizenship if you know why civil service exams are given.

B. WHY ARE CIVIL SERVICE EXAMINATIONS GIVEN?

Civil service examinations are important to you in two ways. As a citizen, you want public jobs filled by employees who know how to do their work. As a job seeker, you want a fair chance to compete for that job on an equal footing with other candidates. The best-known means of accomplishing this two-fold goal is the competitive examination.

Exams are widely publicized throughout the nation. They may be administered for jobs in federal, state, city, municipal, town or village governments or agencies.

Any citizen may apply, with some limitations, such as the age or residence of applicants. Your experience and education may be reviewed to see whether you meet the requirements for the particular examination. When these requirements exist, they are reasonable and applied consistently to all applicants. Thus, a competitive examination may cause you some uneasiness now, but it is your privilege and safeguard.

C. HOW ARE CIVIL SERVICE EXAMS DEVELOPED?

Examinations are carefully written by trained technicians who are specialists in the field known as "psychological measurement," in consultation with recognized authorities in the field of work that the test will cover. These experts recommend the subject matter areas or skills to be tested; only those knowledges or skills important to your success on the job are included. The most reliable books and source materials available are used as references. Together, the experts and technicians judge the difficulty level of the questions.

Test technicians know how to phrase questions so that the problem is clearly stated. Their ethics do not permit "trick" or "catch" questions. Questions may have been tried out on sample groups, or subjected to statistical analysis, to determine their usefulness.

Written tests are often used in combination with performance tests, ratings of training and experience, and oral interviews. All of these measures combine to form the best-known means of finding the right person for the right job.

II. HOW TO PASS THE WRITTEN TEST

A. NATURE OF THE EXAMINATION

To prepare intelligently for civil service examinations, you should know how they differ from school examinations you have taken. In school you were assigned certain definite pages to read or subjects to cover. The examination questions were quite detailed and usually emphasized memory. Civil service exams, on the other hand, try to discover your present ability to perform the duties of a position, plus your potentiality to learn these duties. In other words, a civil service exam attempts to predict how successful you will be. Questions cover such a broad area that they cannot be as minute and detailed as school exam questions.

In the public service similar kinds of work, or positions, are grouped together in one "class." This process is known as *position-classification*. All the positions in a class are paid according to the salary range for that class. One class title covers all of these positions, and they are all tested by the same examination.

B. FOUR BASIC STEPS

1) Study the announcement

How, then, can you know what subjects to study? Our best answer is: "Learn as much as possible about the class of positions for which you've applied." The exam will test the knowledge, skills and abilities needed to do the work.

Your most valuable source of information about the position you want is the official exam announcement. This announcement lists the training and experience qualifications. Check these standards and apply only if you come reasonably close to meeting them.

The brief description of the position in the examination announcement offers some clues to the subjects which will be tested. Think about the job itself. Review the duties in your mind. Can you perform them, or are there some in which you are rusty? Fill in the blank spots in your preparation.

Many jurisdictions preview the written test in the exam announcement by including a section called "Knowledge and Abilities Required," "Scope of the Examination," or some similar heading. Here you will find out specifically what fields will be tested.

2) Review your own background

Once you learn in general what the position is all about, and what you need to know to do the work, ask yourself which subjects you already know fairly well and which need improvement. You may wonder whether to concentrate on improving your strong areas or on building some background in your fields of weakness. When the announcement has specified "some knowledge" or "considerable knowledge," or has used adjectives like "beginning principles of..." or "advanced ... methods," you can get a clue as to the number and difficulty of questions to be asked in any given field. More questions, and hence broader coverage, would be included for those subjects which are more important in the work. Now weigh your strengths and weaknesses against the job requirements and prepare accordingly.

3) Determine the level of the position

Another way to tell how intensively you should prepare is to understand the level of the job for which you are applying. Is it the entering level? In other words, is this the position in which beginners in a field of work are hired? Or is it an intermediate or advanced level? Sometimes this is indicated by such words as "Junior" or "Senior" in the class title. Other jurisdictions use Roman numerals to designate the level – Clerk I, Clerk II, for example. The word "Supervisor" sometimes appears in the title. If the level is not indicated by the title, check the description of duties. Will you be working under very close supervision, or will you have responsibility for independent decisions in this work?

4) Choose appropriate study materials

Now that you know the subjects to be examined and the relative amount of each subject to be covered, you can choose suitable study materials. For beginning level jobs, or even advanced ones, if you have a pronounced weakness in some aspect of your training, read a modern, standard textbook in that field. Be sure it is up to date and has general coverage. Such books are normally available at your library, and the librarian will be glad to help you locate one. For entry-level positions, questions of appropriate difficulty are chosen – neither highly advanced questions, nor those too simple. Such questions require careful thought but not advanced training.

If the position for which you are applying is technical or advanced, you will read more advanced, specialized material. If you are already familiar with the basic principles of your field, elementary textbooks would waste your time. Concentrate on advanced textbooks and technical periodicals. Think through the concepts and review difficult problems in your field.

These are all general sources. You can get more ideas on your own initiative, following these leads. For example, training manuals and publications of the government agency which employs workers in your field can be useful, particularly for technical and professional positions. A letter or visit to the government department involved may result in more specific study suggestions, and certainly will provide you with a more definite idea of the exact nature of the position you are seeking.

III. KINDS OF TESTS

Tests are used for purposes other than measuring knowledge and ability to perform specified duties. For some positions, it is equally important to test ability to make adjustments to new situations or to profit from training. In others, basic mental abilities not dependent on information are essential. Questions which test these things may not appear as pertinent to the duties of the position as those which test for knowledge and information. Yet they are often highly important parts of a fair examination. For very general questions, it is almost impossible to help you direct your study efforts. What we can do is to point out some of the more common of these general abilities needed in public service positions and describe some typical questions.

1) General information

Broad, general information has been found useful for predicting job success in some kinds of work. This is tested in a variety of ways, from vocabulary lists to questions about current events. Basic background in some field of work, such as sociology or economics, may be sampled in a group of questions. Often these are principles which have become familiar to most persons through exposure rather than through formal training. It is difficult to advise you how to study for these questions; being alert to the world around you is our best suggestion.

2) Verbal ability

An example of an ability needed in many positions is verbal or language ability. Verbal ability is, in brief, the ability to use and understand words. Vocabulary and grammar tests are typical measures of this ability. Reading comprehension or paragraph interpretation questions are common in many kinds of civil service tests. You are given a paragraph of written material and asked to find its central meaning.

3) Numerical ability

Number skills can be tested by the familiar arithmetic problem, by checking paired lists of numbers to see which are alike and which are different, or by interpreting charts and graphs. In the latter test, a graph may be printed in the test booklet which you are asked to use as the basis for answering questions.

4) Observation

A popular test for law-enforcement positions is the observation test. A picture is shown to you for several minutes, then taken away. Questions about the picture test your ability to observe both details and larger elements.

5) Following directions

In many positions in the public service, the employee must be able to carry out written instructions dependably and accurately. You may be given a chart with several columns, each column listing a variety of information. The questions require you to carry out directions involving the information given in the chart.

6) Skills and aptitudes

Performance tests effectively measure some manual skills and aptitudes. When the skill is one in which you are trained, such as typing or shorthand, you can practice. These tests are often very much like those given in business school or high school courses. For many of the other skills and aptitudes, however, no short-time preparation can be made. Skills and abilities natural to you or that you have developed throughout your lifetime are being tested.

Many of the general questions just described provide all the data needed to answer the questions and ask you to use your reasoning ability to find the answers. Your best preparation for these tests, as well as for tests of facts and ideas, is to be at your physical and mental best. You, no doubt, have your own methods of getting into an exam-taking mood and keeping "in shape." The next section lists some ideas on this subject.

IV. KINDS OF QUESTIONS

Only rarely is the "essay" question, which you answer in narrative form, used in civil service tests. Civil service tests are usually of the short-answer type. Full instructions for answering these questions will be given to you at the examination. But in case this is your first experience with short-answer questions and separate answer sheets, here is what you need to know:

1) Multiple-choice Questions

Most popular of the short-answer questions is the "multiple choice" or "best answer" question. It can be used, for example, to test for factual knowledge, ability to solve problems or judgment in meeting situations found at work.

A multiple-choice question is normally one of three types—
- It can begin with an incomplete statement followed by several possible endings. You are to find the one ending which *best* completes the statement, although some of the others may not be entirely wrong.
- It can also be a complete statement in the form of a question which is answered by choosing one of the statements listed.

- It can be in the form of a problem – again you select the best answer.

Here is an example of a multiple-choice question with a discussion which should give you some clues as to the method for choosing the right answer:

When an employee has a complaint about his assignment, the action which will *best* help him overcome his difficulty is to
  A. discuss his difficulty with his coworkers
  B. take the problem to the head of the organization
  C. take the problem to the person who gave him the assignment
  D. say nothing to anyone about his complaint

In answering this question, you should study each of the choices to find which is best. Consider choice "A" – Certainly an employee may discuss his complaint with fellow employees, but no change or improvement can result, and the complaint remains unresolved. Choice "B" is a poor choice since the head of the organization probably does not know what assignment you have been given, and taking your problem to him is known as "going over the head" of the supervisor. The supervisor, or person who made the assignment, is the person who can clarify it or correct any injustice. Choice "C" is, therefore, correct. To say nothing, as in choice "D," is unwise. Supervisors have and interest in knowing the problems employees are facing, and the employee is seeking a solution to his problem.

2) True/False Questions

The "true/false" or "right/wrong" form of question is sometimes used. Here a complete statement is given. Your job is to decide whether the statement is right or wrong.

SAMPLE: A roaming cell-phone call to a nearby city costs less than a non-roaming call to a distant city.

This statement is wrong, or false, since roaming calls are more expensive.

This is not a complete list of all possible question forms, although most of the others are variations of these common types. You will always get complete directions for answering questions. Be sure you understand *how* to mark your answers – ask questions until you do.

V. RECORDING YOUR ANSWERS

Computer terminals are used more and more today for many different kinds of exams.
For an examination with very few applicants, you may be told to record your answers in the test booklet itself. Separate answer sheets are much more common. If this separate answer sheet is to be scored by machine – and this is often the case – it is highly important that you mark your answers correctly in order to get credit.
An electronic scoring machine is often used in civil service offices because of the speed with which papers can be scored. Machine-scored answer sheets must be marked with a pencil, which will be given to you. This pencil has a high graphite content which responds to the electronic scoring machine. As a matter of fact, stray dots may register as answers, so do not let your pencil rest on the answer sheet while you are pondering the correct answer. Also, if your pencil lead breaks or is otherwise defective, ask for another.

Since the answer sheet will be dropped in a slot in the scoring machine, be careful not to bend the corners or get the paper crumpled.

The answer sheet normally has five vertical columns of numbers, with 30 numbers to a column. These numbers correspond to the question numbers in your test booklet. After each number, going across the page are four or five pairs of dotted lines. These short dotted lines have small letters or numbers above them. The first two pairs may also have a "T" or "F" above the letters. This indicates that the first two pairs only are to be used if the questions are of the true-false type. If the questions are multiple choice, disregard the "T" and "F" and pay attention only to the small letters or numbers.

Answer your questions in the manner of the sample that follows:

32. The largest city in the United States is
    A. Washington, D.C.
    B. New York City
    C. Chicago
    D. Detroit
    E. San Francisco

1) Choose the answer you think is best. (New York City is the largest, so "B" is correct.)
2) Find the row of dotted lines numbered the same as the question you are answering. (Find row number 32)
3) Find the pair of dotted lines corresponding to the answer. (Find the pair of lines under the mark "B.")
4) Make a solid black mark between the dotted lines.

VI. BEFORE THE TEST

Common sense will help you find procedures to follow to get ready for an examination. Too many of us, however, overlook these sensible measures. Indeed, nervousness and fatigue have been found to be the most serious reasons why applicants fail to do their best on civil service tests. Here is a list of reminders:

- Begin your preparation early – Don't wait until the last minute to go scurrying around for books and materials or to find out what the position is all about.
- Prepare continuously – An hour a night for a week is better than an all-night cram session. This has been definitely established. What is more, a night a week for a month will return better dividends than crowding your study into a shorter period of time.
- Locate the place of the exam – You have been sent a notice telling you when and where to report for the examination. If the location is in a different town or otherwise unfamiliar to you, it would be well to inquire the best route and learn something about the building.
- Relax the night before the test – Allow your mind to rest. Do not study at all that night. Plan some mild recreation or diversion; then go to bed early and get a good night's sleep.
- Get up early enough to make a leisurely trip to the place for the test – This way unforeseen events, traffic snarls, unfamiliar buildings, etc. will not upset you.
- Dress comfortably – A written test is not a fashion show. You will be known by number and not by name, so wear something comfortable.

- Leave excess paraphernalia at home – Shopping bags and odd bundles will get in your way. You need bring only the items mentioned in the official notice you received; usually everything you need is provided. Do not bring reference books to the exam. They will only confuse those last minutes and be taken away from you when in the test room.
- Arrive somewhat ahead of time – If because of transportation schedules you must get there very early, bring a newspaper or magazine to take your mind off yourself while waiting.
- Locate the examination room – When you have found the proper room, you will be directed to the seat or part of the room where you will sit. Sometimes you are given a sheet of instructions to read while you are waiting. Do not fill out any forms until you are told to do so; just read them and be prepared.
- Relax and prepare to listen to the instructions
- If you have any physical problem that may keep you from doing your best, be sure to tell the test administrator. If you are sick or in poor health, you really cannot do your best on the exam. You can come back and take the test some other time.

VII. AT THE TEST

The day of the test is here and you have the test booklet in your hand. The temptation to get going is very strong. Caution! There is more to success than knowing the right answers. You must know how to identify your papers and understand variations in the type of short-answer question used in this particular examination. Follow these suggestions for maximum results from your efforts:

1) Cooperate with the monitor

The test administrator has a duty to create a situation in which you can be as much at ease as possible. He will give instructions, tell you when to begin, check to see that you are marking your answer sheet correctly, and so on. He is not there to guard you, although he will see that your competitors do not take unfair advantage. He wants to help you do your best.

2) Listen to all instructions

Don't jump the gun! Wait until you understand all directions. In most civil service tests you get more time than you need to answer the questions. So don't be in a hurry. Read each word of instructions until you clearly understand the meaning. Study the examples, listen to all announcements and follow directions. Ask questions if you do not understand what to do.

3) Identify your papers

Civil service exams are usually identified by number only. You will be assigned a number; you must not put your name on your test papers. Be sure to copy your number correctly. Since more than one exam may be given, copy your exact examination title.

4) Plan your time

Unless you are told that a test is a "speed" or "rate of work" test, speed itself is usually not important. Time enough to answer all the questions will be provided, but this does not mean that you have all day. An overall time limit has been set. Divide the total time (in minutes) by the number of questions to determine the approximate time you have for each question.

5) Do not linger over difficult questions

If you come across a difficult question, mark it with a paper clip (useful to have along) and come back to it when you have been through the booklet. One caution if you do this – be sure to skip a number on your answer sheet as well. Check often to be sure that you have not lost your place and that you are marking in the row numbered the same as the question you are answering.

6) Read the questions

Be sure you know what the question asks! Many capable people are unsuccessful because they failed to *read* the questions correctly.

7) Answer all questions

Unless you have been instructed that a penalty will be deducted for incorrect answers, it is better to guess than to omit a question.

8) Speed tests

It is often better NOT to guess on speed tests. It has been found that on timed tests people are tempted to spend the last few seconds before time is called in marking answers at random – without even reading them – in the hope of picking up a few extra points. To discourage this practice, the instructions may warn you that your score will be "corrected" for guessing. That is, a penalty will be applied. The incorrect answers will be deducted from the correct ones, or some other penalty formula will be used.

9) Review your answers

If you finish before time is called, go back to the questions you guessed or omitted to give them further thought. Review other answers if you have time.

10) Return your test materials

If you are ready to leave before others have finished or time is called, take ALL your materials to the monitor and leave quietly. Never take any test material with you. The monitor can discover whose papers are not complete, and taking a test booklet may be grounds for disqualification.

VIII. EXAMINATION TECHNIQUES

1) Read the general instructions carefully. These are usually printed on the first page of the exam booklet. As a rule, these instructions refer to the timing of the examination; the fact that you should not start work until the signal and must stop work at a signal, etc. If there are any *special* instructions, such as a choice of questions to be answered, make sure that you note this instruction carefully.

2) When you are ready to start work on the examination, that is as soon as the signal has been given, read the instructions to each question booklet, underline any key words or phrases, such as *least, best, outline, describe* and the like. In this way you will tend to answer as requested rather than discover on reviewing your paper that you *listed without describing*, that you selected the *worst* choice rather than the *best* choice, etc.

3) If the examination is of the objective or multiple-choice type – that is, each question will also give a series of possible answers: A, B, C or D, and you are called upon to select the best answer and write the letter next to that answer on your answer paper – it is advisable to start answering each question in turn. There may be anywhere from 50 to 100 such questions in the three or four hours allotted and you can see how much time would be taken if you read through all the questions before beginning to answer any. Furthermore, if you come across a question or group of questions which you know would be difficult to answer, it would undoubtedly affect your handling of all the other questions.

4) If the examination is of the essay type and contains but a few questions, it is a moot point as to whether you should read all the questions before starting to answer any one. Of course, if you are given a choice – say five out of seven and the like – then it is essential to read all the questions so you can eliminate the two that are most difficult. If, however, you are asked to answer all the questions, there may be danger in trying to answer the easiest one first because you may find that you will spend too much time on it. The best technique is to answer the first question, then proceed to the second, etc.

5) Time your answers. Before the exam begins, write down the time it started, then add the time allowed for the examination and write down the time it must be completed, then divide the time available somewhat as follows:
   - If 3-1/2 hours are allowed, that would be 210 minutes. If you have 80 objective-type questions, that would be an average of 2-1/2 minutes per question. Allow yourself no more than 2 minutes per question, or a total of 160 minutes, which will permit about 50 minutes to review.
   - If for the time allotment of 210 minutes there are 7 essay questions to answer, that would average about 30 minutes a question. Give yourself only 25 minutes per question so that you have about 35 minutes to review.

6) The most important instruction is to *read each question* and make sure you know what is wanted. The second most important instruction is to *time yourself properly* so that you answer every question. The third most important instruction is to *answer every question*. Guess if you have to but include something for each question. Remember that you will receive no credit for a blank and will probably receive some credit if you write something in answer to an essay question. If you guess a letter – say "B" for a multiple-choice question – you may have guessed right. If you leave a blank as an answer to a multiple-choice question, the examiners may respect your feelings but it will not add a point to your score. Some exams may penalize you for wrong answers, so in such cases *only*, you may not want to guess unless you have some basis for your answer.

7) Suggestions
   a. Objective-type questions
      1. Examine the question booklet for proper sequence of pages and questions
      2. Read all instructions carefully
      3. Skip any question which seems too difficult; return to it after all other questions have been answered
      4. Apportion your time properly; do not spend too much time on any single question or group of questions

5. Note and underline key words – *all, most, fewest, least, best, worst, same, opposite*, etc.
6. Pay particular attention to negatives
7. Note unusual option, e.g., unduly long, short, complex, different or similar in content to the body of the question
8. Observe the use of "hedging" words – *probably, may, most likely*, etc.
9. Make sure that your answer is put next to the same number as the question
10. Do not second-guess unless you have good reason to believe the second answer is definitely more correct
11. Cross out original answer if you decide another answer is more accurate; do not erase until you are ready to hand your paper in
12. Answer all questions; guess unless instructed otherwise
13. Leave time for review

   b. Essay questions
     1. Read each question carefully
     2. Determine exactly what is wanted. Underline key words or phrases.
     3. Decide on outline or paragraph answer
     4. Include many different points and elements unless asked to develop any one or two points or elements
     5. Show impartiality by giving pros and cons unless directed to select one side only
     6. Make and write down any assumptions you find necessary to answer the questions
     7. Watch your English, grammar, punctuation and choice of words
     8. Time your answers; don't crowd material

8) Answering the essay question

Most essay questions can be answered by framing the specific response around several key words or ideas. Here are a few such key words or ideas:

M's: manpower, materials, methods, money, management
P's: purpose, program, policy, plan, procedure, practice, problems, pitfalls, personnel, public relations

   a. Six basic steps in handling problems:
     1. Preliminary plan and background development
     2. Collect information, data and facts
     3. Analyze and interpret information, data and facts
     4. Analyze and develop solutions as well as make recommendations
     5. Prepare report and sell recommendations
     6. Install recommendations and follow up effectiveness

   b. Pitfalls to avoid
     1. *Taking things for granted* – A statement of the situation does not necessarily imply that each of the elements is necessarily true; for example, a complaint may be invalid and biased so that all that can be taken for granted is that a complaint has been registered

2. *Considering only one side of a situation* – Wherever possible, indicate several alternatives and then point out the reasons you selected the best one
3. *Failing to indicate follow up* – Whenever your answer indicates action on your part, make certain that you will take proper follow-up action to see how successful your recommendations, procedures or actions turn out to be
4. *Taking too long in answering any single question* – Remember to time your answers properly

IX. AFTER THE TEST

Scoring procedures differ in detail among civil service jurisdictions although the general principles are the same. Whether the papers are hand-scored or graded by machine we have described, they are nearly always graded by number. That is, the person who marks the paper knows only the number – never the name – of the applicant. Not until all the papers have been graded will they be matched with names. If other tests, such as training and experience or oral interview ratings have been given, scores will be combined. Different parts of the examination usually have different weights. For example, the written test might count 60 percent of the final grade, and a rating of training and experience 40 percent. In many jurisdictions, veterans will have a certain number of points added to their grades.

After the final grade has been determined, the names are placed in grade order and an eligible list is established. There are various methods for resolving ties between those who get the same final grade – probably the most common is to place first the name of the person whose application was received first. Job offers are made from the eligible list in the order the names appear on it. You will be notified of your grade and your rank as soon as all these computations have been made. This will be done as rapidly as possible.

People who are found to meet the requirements in the announcement are called "eligibles." Their names are put on a list of eligible candidates. An eligible's chances of getting a job depend on how high he stands on this list and how fast agencies are filling jobs from the list.

When a job is to be filled from a list of eligibles, the agency asks for the names of people on the list of eligibles for that job. When the civil service commission receives this request, it sends to the agency the names of the three people highest on this list. Or, if the job to be filled has specialized requirements, the office sends the agency the names of the top three persons who meet these requirements from the general list.

The appointing officer makes a choice from among the three people whose names were sent to him. If the selected person accepts the appointment, the names of the others are put back on the list to be considered for future openings.

That is the rule in hiring from all kinds of eligible lists, whether they are for typist, carpenter, chemist, or something else. For every vacancy, the appointing officer has his choice of any one of the top three eligibles on the list. This explains why the person whose name is on top of the list sometimes does not get an appointment when some of the persons lower on the list do. If the appointing officer chooses the second or third eligible, the No. 1 eligible does not get a job at once, but stays on the list until he is appointed or the list is terminated.

X. HOW TO PASS THE INTERVIEW TEST

The examination for which you applied requires an oral interview test. You have already taken the written test and you are now being called for the interview test – the final part of the formal examination.

You may think that it is not possible to prepare for an interview test and that there are no procedures to follow during an interview. Our purpose is to point out some things you can do in advance that will help you and some good rules to follow and pitfalls to avoid while you are being interviewed.

What is an interview supposed to test?

The written examination is designed to test the technical knowledge and competence of the candidate; the oral is designed to evaluate intangible qualities, not readily measured otherwise, and to establish a list showing the relative fitness of each candidate – as measured against his competitors – for the position sought. Scoring is not on the basis of "right" and "wrong," but on a sliding scale of values ranging from "not passable" to "outstanding." As a matter of fact, it is possible to achieve a relatively low score without a single "incorrect" answer because of evident weakness in the qualities being measured.

Occasionally, an examination may consist entirely of an oral test – either an individual or a group oral. In such cases, information is sought concerning the technical knowledges and abilities of the candidate, since there has been no written examination for this purpose. More commonly, however, an oral test is used to supplement a written examination.

Who conducts interviews?

The composition of oral boards varies among different jurisdictions. In nearly all, a representative of the personnel department serves as chairman. One of the members of the board may be a representative of the department in which the candidate would work. In some cases, "outside experts" are used, and, frequently, a businessman or some other representative of the general public is asked to serve. Labor and management or other special groups may be represented. The aim is to secure the services of experts in the appropriate field.

However the board is composed, it is a good idea (and not at all improper or unethical) to ascertain in advance of the interview who the members are and what groups they represent. When you are introduced to them, you will have some idea of their backgrounds and interests, and at least you will not stutter and stammer over their names.

What should be done before the interview?

While knowledge about the board members is useful and takes some of the surprise element out of the interview, there is other preparation which is more substantive. It *is* possible to prepare for an oral interview – in several ways:

1) Keep a copy of your application and review it carefully before the interview

This may be the only document before the oral board, and the starting point of the interview. Know what education and experience you have listed there, and the sequence and dates of all of it. Sometimes the board will ask you to review the highlights of your experience for them; you should not have to hem and haw doing it.

2) Study the class specification and the examination announcement

Usually, the oral board has one or both of these to guide them. The qualities, characteristics or knowledges required by the position sought are stated in these documents. They offer valuable clues as to the nature of the oral interview. For example, if the job involves supervisory responsibilities, the announcement will usually indicate that knowledge of modern supervisory methods and the qualifications of the candidate as a supervisor will be tested. If so, you can expect such questions, frequently in the form of a hypothetical situation which you are expected to solve. NEVER go into an oral without knowledge of the duties and responsibilities of the job you seek.

3) Think through each qualification required

Try to visualize the kind of questions you would ask if you were a board member. How well could you answer them? Try especially to appraise your own knowledge and background in each area, *measured against the job sought*, and identify any areas in which you are weak. Be critical and realistic – do not flatter yourself.

4) Do some general reading in areas in which you feel you may be weak

For example, if the job involves supervision and your past experience has NOT, some general reading in supervisory methods and practices, particularly in the field of human relations, might be useful. Do NOT study agency procedures or detailed manuals. The oral board will be testing your understanding and capacity, not your memory.

5) Get a good night's sleep and watch your general health and mental attitude

You will want a clear head at the interview. Take care of a cold or any other minor ailment, and of course, no hangovers.

What should be done on the day of the interview?

Now comes the day of the interview itself. Give yourself plenty of time to get there. Plan to arrive somewhat ahead of the scheduled time, particularly if your appointment is in the fore part of the day. If a previous candidate fails to appear, the board might be ready for you a bit early. By early afternoon an oral board is almost invariably behind schedule if there are many candidates, and you may have to wait. Take along a book or magazine to read, or your application to review, but leave any extraneous material in the waiting room when you go in for your interview. In any event, relax and compose yourself.

The matter of dress is important. The board is forming impressions about you – from your experience, your manners, your attitude, and your appearance. Give your personal appearance careful attention. Dress your best, but not your flashiest. Choose conservative, appropriate clothing, and be sure it is immaculate. This is a business interview, and your appearance should indicate that you regard it as such. Besides, being well groomed and properly dressed will help boost your confidence.

Sooner or later, someone will call your name and escort you into the interview room. *This is it.* From here on you are on your own. It is too late for any more preparation. But remember, you asked for this opportunity to prove your fitness, and you are here because your request was granted.

What happens when you go in?

The usual sequence of events will be as follows: The clerk (who is often the board stenographer) will introduce you to the chairman of the oral board, who will introduce you to the other members of the board. Acknowledge the introductions before you sit down. Do not be surprised if you find a microphone facing you or a stenotypist sitting by. Oral interviews are usually recorded in the event of an appeal or other review.

Usually the chairman of the board will open the interview by reviewing the highlights of your education and work experience from your application – primarily for the benefit of the other members of the board, as well as to get the material into the record. Do not interrupt or comment unless there is an error or significant misinterpretation; if that is the case, do not hesitate. But do not quibble about insignificant matters. Also, he will usually ask you some question about your education, experience or your present job – partly to get you to start talking and to establish the interviewing "rapport." He may start the actual questioning, or turn it over to one of the other members. Frequently, each member undertakes the questioning on a particular area, one in which he is perhaps most competent, so you can expect each member to participate in the examination. Because time is limited, you may also expect some rather abrupt switches in the direction the questioning takes, so do not be upset by it. Normally, a board member will not pursue a single line of questioning unless he discovers a particular strength or weakness.

After each member has participated, the chairman will usually ask whether any member has any further questions, then will ask you if you have anything you wish to add. Unless you are expecting this question, it may floor you. Worse, it may start you off on an extended, extemporaneous speech. The board is not usually seeking more information. The question is principally to offer you a last opportunity to present further qualifications or to indicate that you have nothing to add. So, if you feel that a significant qualification or characteristic has been overlooked, it is proper to point it out in a sentence or so. Do not compliment the board on the thoroughness of their examination – they have been sketchy, and you know it. If you wish, merely say, "No thank you, I have nothing further to add." This is a point where you can "talk yourself out" of a good impression or fail to present an important bit of information. Remember, *you close the interview yourself.*

The chairman will then say, "That is all, Mr. _____, thank you." Do not be startled; the interview is over, and quicker than you think. Thank him, gather your belongings and take your leave. Save your sigh of relief for the other side of the door.

How to put your best foot forward

Throughout this entire process, you may feel that the board individually and collectively is trying to pierce your defenses, seek out your hidden weaknesses and embarrass and confuse you. Actually, this is not true. They are obliged to make an appraisal of your qualifications for the job you are seeking, and they want to see you in your best light. Remember, they must interview all candidates and a non-cooperative candidate may become a failure in spite of their best efforts to bring out his qualifications. Here are 15 suggestions that will help you:

1) Be natural – Keep your attitude confident, not cocky

If you are not confident that you can do the job, do not expect the board to be. Do not apologize for your weaknesses, try to bring out your strong points. The board is interested in a positive, not negative, presentation. Cockiness will antagonize any board member and make him wonder if you are covering up a weakness by a false show of strength.

2) Get comfortable, but don't lounge or sprawl

Sit erectly but not stiffly. A careless posture may lead the board to conclude that you are careless in other things, or at least that you are not impressed by the importance of the occasion. Either conclusion is natural, even if incorrect. Do not fuss with your clothing, a pencil or an ashtray. Your hands may occasionally be useful to emphasize a point; do not let them become a point of distraction.

3) Do not wisecrack or make small talk

This is a serious situation, and your attitude should show that you consider it as such. Further, the time of the board is limited – they do not want to waste it, and neither should you.

4) Do not exaggerate your experience or abilities
   In the first place, from information in the application or other interviews and sources, the board may know more about you than you think. Secondly, you probably will not get away with it. An experienced board is rather adept at spotting such a situation, so do not take the chance.

5) If you know a board member, do not make a point of it, yet do not hide it
   Certainly you are not fooling him, and probably not the other members of the board. Do not try to take advantage of your acquaintanceship – it will probably do you little good.

6) Do not dominate the interview
   Let the board do that. They will give you the clues – do not assume that you have to do all the talking. Realize that the board has a number of questions to ask you, and do not try to take up all the interview time by showing off your extensive knowledge of the answer to the first one.

7) Be attentive
   You only have 20 minutes or so, and you should keep your attention at its sharpest throughout. When a member is addressing a problem or question to you, give him your undivided attention. Address your reply principally to him, but do not exclude the other board members.

8) Do not interrupt
   A board member may be stating a problem for you to analyze. He will ask you a question when the time comes. Let him state the problem, and wait for the question.

9) Make sure you understand the question
   Do not try to answer until you are sure what the question is. If it is not clear, restate it in your own words or ask the board member to clarify it for you. However, do not haggle about minor elements.

10) Reply promptly but not hastily
   A common entry on oral board rating sheets is "candidate responded readily," or "candidate hesitated in replies." Respond as promptly and quickly as you can, but do not jump to a hasty, ill-considered answer.

11) Do not be peremptory in your answers
   A brief answer is proper – but do not fire your answer back. That is a losing game from your point of view. The board member can probably ask questions much faster than you can answer them.

12) Do not try to create the answer you think the board member wants
   He is interested in what kind of mind you have and how it works – not in playing games. Furthermore, he can usually spot this practice and will actually grade you down on it.

13) Do not switch sides in your reply merely to agree with a board member
   Frequently, a member will take a contrary position merely to draw you out and to see if you are willing and able to defend your point of view. Do not start a debate, yet do not surrender a good position. If a position is worth taking, it is worth defending.

14) Do not be afraid to admit an error in judgment if you are shown to be wrong

The board knows that you are forced to reply without any opportunity for careful consideration. Your answer may be demonstrably wrong. If so, admit it and get on with the interview.

15) Do not dwell at length on your present job

The opening question may relate to your present assignment. Answer the question but do not go into an extended discussion. You are being examined for a *new* job, not your present one. As a matter of fact, try to phrase ALL your answers in terms of the job for which you are being examined.

Basis of Rating

Probably you will forget most of these "do's" and "don'ts" when you walk into the oral interview room. Even remembering them all will not ensure you a passing grade. Perhaps you did not have the qualifications in the first place. But remembering them will help you to put your best foot forward, without treading on the toes of the board members.

Rumor and popular opinion to the contrary notwithstanding, an oral board wants you to make the best appearance possible. They know you are under pressure – but they also want to see how you respond to it as a guide to what your reaction would be under the pressures of the job you seek. They will be influenced by the degree of poise you display, the personal traits you show and the manner in which you respond.

ABOUT THIS BOOK

This book contains tests divided into Examination Sections. Go through each test, answering every question in the margin. We have also attached a sample answer sheet at the back of the book that can be removed and used. At the end of each test look at the answer key and check your answers. On the ones you got wrong, look at the right answer choice and learn. Do not fill in the answers first. Do not memorize the questions and answers, but understand the answer and principles involved. On your test, the questions will likely be different from the samples. Questions are changed and new ones added. If you understand these past questions you should have success with any changes that arise. Tests may consist of several types of questions. We have additional books on each subject should more study be advisable or necessary for you. Finally, the more you study, the better prepared you will be. This book is intended to be the last thing you study before you walk into the examination room. Prior study of relevant texts is also recommended. NLC publishes some of these in our Fundamental Series. Knowledge and good sense are important factors in passing your exam. Good luck also helps. So now study this Passbook, absorb the material contained within and take that knowledge into the examination. Then do your best to pass that exam.

EXAMINATION SECTION

EXAMINATION SECTION
TEST 1

DIRECTIONS: Each question or incomplete statement is followed by several suggested answers or completions. Select the one that BEST answers the question or completes the statement. *PRINT THE LETTER OF THE CORRECT ANSWER IN THE SPACE AT THE RIGHT.*

1. Of the following statements relating to new bell and spigot pipe being laid in a trench, the one that is CORRECT is that

    A. the enlarged end of the pipe faces downstream
    B. bell and spigot pipe is usually elliptical in shape
    C. when building a new line using bell and spigot pipe, you start from the downstream end
    D. vitrified pipe is usually thicker than concrete pipe of the same diameter

    1._____

2. Vitrified pipe is made of

    A. clay   B. vermiculite
    C. gypsum   D. Portland cement

    2._____

3. The invert of a sewer pipe is its

    A. outer top   B. inner bottom
    C. inner top   D. outer bottom

    3._____

4. A cradle is usually placed under a sewer pipe when the

    A. trench is narrow   B. trench is wide
    C. soil is poor   D. pipe is near the surface

    4._____

5. A monolithic sewer is a

    A. vitrified pipe sewer
    B. sewer carrying only storm water
    C. cast-iron sewer containing bell and spigot joints
    D. reinforced concrete cast-in-place sewer

    5._____

6. Of the following, the BEST reason for placing manholes on sewers is to

    A. provide access for inspection and maintenance
    B. allow for overflow during a heavy storm
    C. pinpoint the location of the sewer
    D. give access to the sewer for the purpose of snow removal

    6._____

7. The sheeting in a trench for a sheeted sewer is ordered left in place after the sewer has been built and backfilled. The BEST reason for ordering the sheeting left in place is that

    A. the sheeting is too expensive to remove
    B. the removal of the sheeting would disturb the sewer
    C. this minimizes the settlement outside the sheeted area
    D. the sheeting is too difficult to remove

    7._____

8. The two MOST frequently used types of sheeting for normal soil conditions and average depths are

   A. soldier beams with horizontal sheeting and vertical wood sheeting with bracing
   B. steel sheet piling and vertical wood sheeting
   C. precast concrete planks with soldier beams and steel sheet piling
   D. slurry walls and vertical wood sheeting

9. A specification for a new sewer requires that the pavement NOT be restored for a period of at least six months after the backfill is in place.
   The BEST reason for this requirement is to

   A. be sure that the sewer will work before restoring the pavement
   B. minimize the settlement of the pavement
   C. defer final payment to the contractor
   D. allow the use of a lighter pavement

10. In reinforced concrete sewers, the reinforcing steel must have a minimum cover of concrete.
    Of the following, the BEST reason for this requirement is to

    A. make the sewer watertight
    B. protect the reinforcing steel against corrosion
    C. allow the use of smaller sized stone in the concrete
    D. eliminate the need for vibrating concrete

11. As used in relation to sewers, infiltration refers to the

    A. leakage of sewage from the sewer to the surrounding soil
    B. connection of sanitary sewer lines into storm water sewers
    C. inflow of ground water into the sewer
    D. loss of mortar at the joints of prefabricated sewers

12. A BAD effect of infiltration in a sanitary sewer is that it

    A. tends to overload the sewage treatment plant
    B. corrodes the sewer
    C. causes cavitation in the sewer
    D. increases the carrying capacity of the sewer

13. A storm sewer GENERALLY differs from a sanitary sewer in that a storm sewer

    A. is generally larger in size than a sanitary sewer and carries little dry-weather flow
    B. is generally made of concrete whereas a sanitary sewer is generally made of cast iron
    C. generally requires fewer manholes than a sanitary sewer
    D. generally has a large slope whereas a sanitary sewer generally has a small slope

14. Manhole frames and covers are USUALLY made of

    A. aluminum   B. malleable iron
    C. cast iron   D. steel

15. The spacing of rungs used for steps in a manhole is MOST NEARLY _____ inches.   15._____
    A. 4   B. 12   C. 20   D. 26

16. Steel is galvanized by coating it with   16._____
    A. tin   B. lead   C. copper   D. zinc

17. The reinforcing steel in a cast-in-place concrete sewer section would MOST likely be placed as shown in   17._____

    A.   B.

    C.   D.

18. Well points would MOST likely be used in the construction of a sewer when the   18._____
    A. sewer is very deep
    B. sewer is in rock
    C. soil is clayey
    D. water table is above the sewer

19. The purpose of jetting the well points in sewer construction is to   19._____
    A. clean out the screen
    B. set the well point in place
    C. clean out the area outside the screen
    D. remove water from the surrounding area

20. The type of soil in which well points operate MOST efficiently is   20._____
    A. sand   B. clay   C. rock   D. silt

21. The water-cement ratio of a concrete mix is USUALLY expressed in terms of   21._____
    A. barrels of cement per gallon of water
    B. bags of cement per gallon of water
    C. gallons of water per bag of cement
    D. gallons of water per barrel of cement

22. The effective diameter of a number 4 reinforcing bar is MOST NEARLY _____ inch.

    A. 1/4   B. 1/2   C. 3/4   D. 1

23. The PRIMARY purpose of curing freshly poured concrete is to

    A. keep the surface smooth
    B. prevent honeycombing of the surface
    C. improve the appearance of the surface
    D. prevent evaporation of water from the surface

24. A bag of cement weighs MOST NEARLY _____ pounds.

    A. 94   B. 104   C. 114   D. 124

25. Of the following, the material that may be used as the coarse aggregate in ordinary Portland cement concrete is

    A. well graded sand   B. sand of uniform size
    C. crushed rock   D. micaschist

26. In a 1:2:4 concrete mix, the 2 stands for the quantity of

    A. water   B. fine aggregate
    C. coarse aggregate   D. cement

27. The height of a slump cone used in concrete testing is _____ inches.

    A. 6   B. 8   C. 10   D. 12

28. As commonly used, 3000-pound concrete refers to 3000 pounds per

    A. inch   B. square inch
    C. cubic inch   D. foot

29. The factor that has the GREATEST effect on the strength of concrete is the

    A. size of coarse aggregate
    B. uniformity of the aggregate
    C. water-cement ratio
    D. quality of the fine aggregate

30. The number of bags of cement needed to produce a cubic yard of concrete is called the _____ factor.

    A. cement   B. yield   C. bulk   D. output

31. The MAIN purpose of vibrating newly poured concrete when it is in the forms is to

    A. remove high points on the surface
    B. eliminate air pockets on the surface
    C. remove excess water
    D. distribute the aggregate evenly in the concrete

32. A cubic foot of ordinary Portland cement concrete weighs MOST NEARLY _____ pounds.

    A. 145   B. 165   C. 195   D. 220

33. The MAIN purpose of adding an air entraining agent to a concrete mix used for sidewalks is to 33.____

    A. improve the resistance of the concrete to freezing and thawing conditions
    B. decrease the weight of the concrete to lighten the dead load of the concrete
    C. increase the compressive strength of the concrete
    D. decrease the resistance of the concrete to bleeding

34. Of the following operations on a fresh concrete surface, the one that should be performed FIRST is 34.____

    A. screeding   B. floating
    C. trowelling   D. brooming

35. When concrete is referred to as *3000-pound concrete*, the *3000* refers to its strength at the end of _____ days. 35.____

    A. 7   B. 14   C. 21   D. 28

KEY (CORRECT ANSWERS)

1. C		16. D	
2. A		17. A	
3. B		18. D	
4. C		19. B	
5. D		20. A	
6. A		21. C	
7. C		22. B	
8. A		23. D	
9. B		24. A	
10. B		25. C	
11. C		26. B	
12. A		27. D	
13. A		28. B	
14. C		29. C	
15. B		30. A	

31. B
32. A
33. A
34. A
35. D

TEST 2

DIRECTIONS: Each question or incomplete statement is followed by several suggested answers or completions. Select the one that BEST answers the question or completes the statement. *PRINT THE LETTER OF THE CORRECT ANSWER IN THE SPACE AT THE RIGHT.*

1. If a batch of concrete is very stiff, its MAIN characteristic is that it

   A. has a low slump
   B. has a high slump
   C. is undersanded
   D. is oversanded

2. Reinforcing steel should have the GREATEST cover of concrete when the concrete surface is

   A. in contact with the ground
   B. in contact with outside air
   C. an interior wall
   D. an interior ceiling

3. The MAIN difference between reinforced concrete and plain concrete is that plain concrete uses _____ for reinforcing.

   A. larger aggregate
   B. high early strength cement
   C. steel
   D. a low water-cement ratio

4. Of the following types of wood, the one that would MOST likely be used in form work for concrete is

   A. oak   B. maple   C. fir   D. birch

5. The size that SEPARATES the fine aggregate from the coarse aggregate in a concrete mix is _____ inch.

   A. 1/8   B. 1/4   C. 3/8   D. 1/2

6. The MINIMUM thickness of sidewalk pavements for pedes-trian use should be _____ inches.

   A. 4   B. 5   C. 6   D. 7

7. An ADVANTAGE of using sand instead of salt on concrete roadway surfaces when snow and ice settle on them is that sand

   A. is easier to remove than salt when the snow disappears
   B. will harm catch basins less than salt when the materials are washed into the catch basin
   C. will not harm the concrete surface whereas salt is harmful to the surface
   D. will help melt the surface ice whereas salt will have no effect on the ice on the surface

8. Sidewalks should be pitched toward the street at a MINIMUM of _____ inch per _____.

   A. 1/8; foot B. 1/8; yard
   C. 5/8; foot D. 1; foot

9. A freshly poured concrete sidewalk is usually finished with a

   A. screed   B. wood float
   C. steel trowel D. darby

10.

    The shape of the roadway section shown above is USUALLY a(n)

    A. circle B. ellipse C. parabola D. hyperbola

11. The MAIN advantage of using large coarse aggregate in a concrete mix is that

    A. the mix is more workable
    B. the mix is stronger
    C. there is a saving in cement
    D. less water is required

12. In building a new street, sidewalk, and curb in a previously unpaved area, the order of construction practically ALWAYS followed is that the

    A. sidewalk precedes the road pavement
    B. sidewalk follows the road pavement
    C. curb precedes the road pavement
    D. road pavement precedes the curb

13. The USUAL range of depth of a curb from top surface of road at curb to top of curb is _____ inches to _____ inches.

    A. 4; 8 B. 8; 12 C. 12; 16 D. 16; 20

14. The dimensions of common brick are GENERALLY

    A. 2 1/4" x 2 3/4" x 12"   B. 2 1/4" x 3 3/4" x 8"
    C. 2 3/4" x 3 3/4" x 8"   D. 2 3/4" x 4 3/4" x 12"

15. Common brick is made of

    A. limestone B. sand C. clay D. loess

16. Carbon black is added to concrete to

    A. give the concrete a black color
    B. accelerate the setting of the concrete
    C. retard the setting of the concrete
    D. improve the workability of the concrete

17. When steel curb angles are used for curbs, anchors are attached, to the curb angles. The MAIN purpose of the anchors is to

   A. hold the curb in place when the curb is being poured
   B. bond the curb angle into the concrete curb
   C. anchor the curb angle into the soil
   D. anchor the curb angle into the sidewalk

17.____

18. Wire mesh is specified in pounds per

   A. square foot
   B. square yard
   C. hundred square feet
   D. hundred square yards

18.____

19.

   An asphalt pavement consists of three layers.
   The layer marked E in the sketch above is the _____ course.

   A. tack   B. binder   C. base   D. wearing

19.____

20. The BASE course of a sheet asphalt pavement is usually made of

   A. sheet asphalt
   B. concrete
   C. tar
   D. bituminous binder

20.____

21. In asphalt paving, the tack coat is USUALLY applied

   A. on the finished wearing surface
   B. on the surface of the soil to receive the pavement
   C. on hard dense impervious surfaces
   D. along the curb

21.____

22. The specification for a pavement states that the penetration of asphalt is measured in units of mm.
   This stands for

   A. micrometer
   B. macrometer
   C. manometer
   D. millimeter

22.____

23. In an asphalt pavement, the LIQUID part of the asphalt mix is

   A. bitumen   B. water   C. gasoline   D. benzene

23.____

24. The terms liquid limit, plastic limit, and plasticity index refer to tests on

   A. asphalt   B. soil   C. concrete   D. gravel

24.____

25. For a bituminous paving material, sieves and sieve analysis are used to analyze the

   A. cement   B. aggregate   C. clay   D. silt

25.____

26. The size of sidewalk panels is USUALLY

   A. 2' x 2'   B. 3' x 3'   C. 5' x 5'   D. 6' x 6'

26.____

27. The slope of a sidewalk is designated as 2 inches in 5 feet.
The drop in elevation of the sidewalk in 30' is _____ foot.

    A. one   B. 1/2 of a   C. 3/4 of a   D. 1/4 of a

27.____

28. In placing temporary asphaltic pavement upon completion of the backfill in a street opening, a 3 inch thick pavement should be laid one inch above the adjoining asphalt permanent pavement.
The MAIN reason for making the temporary pavement one inch above the finished pavement is to

    A. provide adequate drainage
    B. allow for settlement
    C. identify the temporarily paved area
    D. save excavation when the permanent pavement is placed

28.____

29. A maintenance bond for a roadway pavement is in an amount of 10% of the estimated cost.
If the estimated cost is $80,000, the maintenance bond is

    A. $80   B. $800   C. $8,000   D. $80,000

29.____

30. Specifications require that a core be taken every 700 square yards of paved roadway or fraction thereof.
A 100 foot by 200 foot rectangular area would require _____ core(s).

    A. 1   B. 2   C. 3   D. 4

30.____

31. An applicant must file a map at a scale of 1" = 40'.
Six inches on the map represents _____ feet on the ground.

    A. 600   B. 240   C. 120   D. D, 60

31.____

32. A 100' x 110' lot has an area of MOST NEARLY _____ acre.

    A. 1/8   B. 1/4   C. 3/8   D. 1/2

32.____

33. 1 inch is MOST NEARLY equal to _____ feet.

    A. .02   B. .04   C. .06   D. .08

33.____

34. The area of the triangle EFG shown at the right is MOST NEARLY _____ sq.ft.
    A. 36
    B. 42
    C. 48
    D. 54

34.____

35. Specifications state: As further security for the faith-ful performance of this contract, the comptroller shall deduct, and retain until the final payment, 10% of the value of the work certified for payment in each partial payment voucher, until the amount so deducted and retained shall equal 5% of the contract price or in the case of a unit price contract, 5% of the estimated amount to be paid to the contractor under the contract.
For a $300,000 contract, the amount to be retained at the end of the contract is

    A. $5,000   B. $10,000   C. $15,000   D. $20,000

35.____

KEY (CORRECT ANSWERS)

1.	A	16.	A
2.	A	17.	B
3.	A	18.	C
4.	C	19.	B
5.	B	20.	B
6.	A	21.	C
7.	C	22.	D
8.	A	23.	A
9.	B	24.	B
10.	C	25.	B
11.	C	26.	C
12.	C	27.	A
13.	A	28.	B
14.	B	29.	C
15.	C	30.	D

31. B
32. B
33. D
34. A
35. C

TEST 3

DIRECTIONS: Each question or incomplete statement is followed by several suggested answers or completions. Select the one that BEST answers the question or completes the statement. *PRINT THE LETTER OF THE CORRECT ANSWER IN THE SPACE AT THE RIGHT.*

Questions 1-4.

DIRECTIONS: Questions 1 through 4, inclusive, refer to the plan of a sewer shown below.

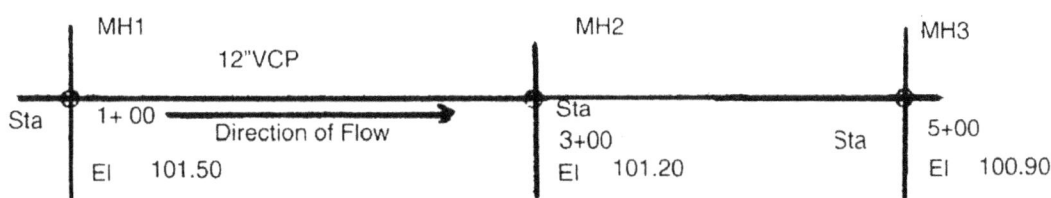

PLAN - SEWER

1. The distance, in feet, between MH1 and MH3 is _____ feet. 1.____
   A. 200 B. 300 C. 400 D. 500

2. The drop in elevation between MH1 and MH3 is 2.____
   A. 0.60' B. 0.50' C. 0.40' D. 0.30'

3. If the scale of the drawing is 1 inch = 40 feet, the length of the line on the plan between MH1 and MH2 should be, in inches, 3.____
   A. 3 B. 4 C. 5 D. 6

4. A vertical section taken along the length of the sewer would be called a 4.____
   A. cross section   B. development
   C. partial plan   D. profile

5. A line joining points of equal elevation on a plan is known as a(n) 5.____
   A. profile B. contour C. elevation D. isobar

6. The Federal agency concerned with safety on a construction site is 6.____
   A. OSHA B. FIDC C. FEMA D. NHOC

7. A Federal safety requirement on construction sites is that 7.____
   A. a nurse must be present at all times
   B. a safety inspector, whose only duty is safety, be assigned full time to construction sites
   C. safety hats must be worn
   D. metal scaffolds are not permitted on the job site

11

8. Safety shoes are shoes that have a(n)

    A. extra heavy sole
    B. extra heavy heel
    C. metal covering the toe
    D. special leather covering over the ankles

9. A material whose use has been curtailed in building and heavy construction is

    A. poured cut asphalt
    B. lightweight concrete aggregate
    C. latex paint
    D. sprayed-on asbestos

10. In making a field report, it is POOR practice to erase information on the report in order to make a change because

    A. there is a question of what was changed and why it was changed
    B. you are liable to erase through the paper and tear the report
    C. the report will no longer look neat and presentable
    D. the duplicate copies will be smudged

11. It is PREFERABLE to print information on a field report rather than write it out longhand mainly because

    A. printing takes less time to write than writing long-hand
    B. printing is usually easier to read than longhand writing
    C. longhand writing on field reports is not acceptable in court cases
    D. printing occupies less space on a report than long hand writing

12. Where the length of roadway pavement is less than 100 lineal feet, the requirement of cores may be waived.
    The term waived in the above statement means MOST NEARLY

    A. eliminated   B. enforced
    C. considered   D. postponed

13. Inspectors are provided with standardized forms, and they have to fill in information as requested on the form.
    Of the following, the MAIN advantage of this type of form is that

    A. the inspector will be less likely to omit important information
    B. it is cheap to print
    C. it is confidential and only authorized people will see it
    D. it is easy to make copies of the form

14. Where only part of the sidewalk is to be relaid, the concrete shall match the predominant color of the existing sidewalk.
    The word predominant in the above sentence means MOST NEARLY

    A. lightest   B. darkest
    C. main   D. contrasting

15. All stands must be substantially built so as not to create any hazard to passersby or other persons.
The word hazard in the above sentence means MOST NEARLY
    A. delay
    B. danger
    C. obstruction
    D. inconvenience

15.____

16. The lights shall be lighted and remain lighted every night during the hours prescribed for public street lamps.
The word prescribed in the above sentence means MOST NEARLY
    A. required
    B. not needed
    C. before midnight
    D. of darkness

16.____

17. The Department of Highways in its discretion may direct that certain regulations be waived.
In the above sentence, the word discretion means MOST NEARLY
    A. jurisdiction
    B. operation
    C. organization
    D. judgment

17.____

18. A sidewalk that abuts a curb _____ the curb.
    A. is above
    B. is below
    C. touches
    D. is integral with

18.____

19. All canopy permits shall be posted in a conspicuous place at the entrance for which the permit is issued.
The word conspicuous means MOST NEARLY
    A. well known
    B. inaccessible
    C. easily observed
    D. obscure

19.____

20. Where a street opening is made by a licensed plumber, a plunber's bond may be filed in lieu of a street obstruction bond.
The words in lieu of mean MOST NEARLY
    A. in addition to
    B. instead of
    C. immediately as
    D. appurtenant to

20.____

21. Of the following characteristics of a written report, the one that is MOST important is its
    A. length
    B. accuracy
    C. organization
    D. grammar

21.____

22. A written report to your superior contains many spelling errors.
Of the following statements relating to spelling errors, the one that is MOST NEARLY correct is that
    A. this is unimportant as long as the meaning of the report is clear
    B. readers of the report will ignore the many spelling errors
    C. readers of the report will get a poor opinion of the writer of the report
    D. spelling errors are unimportant as long as the grammar is correct

22.____

23. Written reports to your superior should have the same general arrangement and layout. The BEST reason for this requirement is that the

   A. report will be more accurate
   B. report will be more complete
   C. person who reads the report will know what the subject of the report is
   D. person who reads the report will know where to look for information in the report

24. The first paragraph of a report usually contains detailed information on the subject of the report.
   Of the following, the BEST reason for this requirement is to enable the

   A. reader to quickly find the subject of the report
   B. typist to immediately determine the subject of the report so that she will understand what she is typing
   C. clerk to determine to whom copies of the report shall be routed
   D. typist to quickly determine how many copies of the report will be needed

Questions 25-26.

DIRECTIONS: Questions 25 and 26 refer to the girder shown in the sketch below.

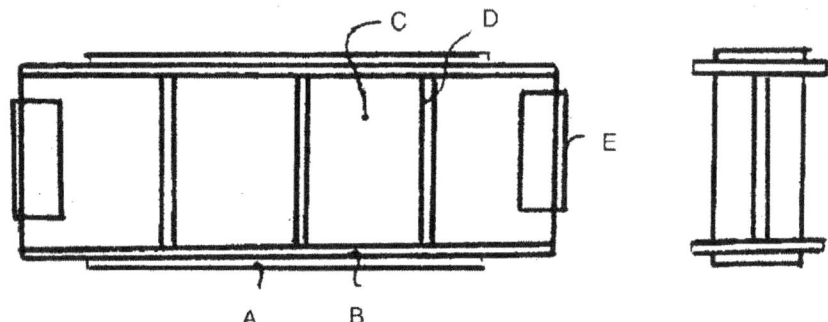

25. A report speaks of stiffeners on girders.
    The stiffener would be the part shown as

    A. A   B. B   C. C   D. D

26. The flange would be the part shown as

    A. E   B. B   C. C   D. D

27. When an inspector is writing a report about a problem your agency handles, the report should contain four major parts: a description of the problem, the location, the details of the problem, and

    A. your recommendation
    B. references to the drawings that pertain to the problem
    C. the borough in which the problem is located
    D. the agency to whom the problem should be referred

28. A report refers to a Pratt truss.
    The material composition of the truss is MOST likely

    A. wood   B. concrete   C. steel   D. aluminum

29. A plumb bob is USUALLY used to   29.____

    A. check grades
    B. establish a vertical line
    C. hold down equipment
    D. check the grading of sand

30. As a general rule, any time a measurement is made in the field, the number of quantity   30.____
    should be immediately recorded.
    Of the following, the BEST reason for immediately recording this information is that

    A. the office is interested in receiving this information as quickly as possible
    B. this enables the inspector to complete his report more quickly
    C. this information may be needed for computations
    D. it is easy to forget or mistake numbers if they are not immediately recorded

---

KEY(CORRECT ANSWERS)

1.	C	16.	A
2.	A	17.	D
3.	C	18.	C
4.	D	19.	C
5.	B	20.	B
6.	A	21.	B
7.	C	22.	C
8.	C	23.	D
9.	D	24.	A
10.	A	25.	D
11.	B	26.	B
12.	A	27.	A
13.	A	28.	C
14.	C	29.	B
15.	B	30.	D

EXAMINATION SECTION
TEST 1

DIRECTIONS: Each question or incomplete statement is followed by several suggested answers or completions. Select the one that BEST answers the question or completes the statement. *PRINT THE LETTER OF THE CORRECT ANSWER IN THE SPACE AT THE RIGHT.*

1. Asphalt is derived mainly

    A. as a byproduct from the production of coke
    B. from asphalt deposits seeping to the surface of the earth
    C. from the refining of crude oil
    D. from bituminous coal

    1.____

2. Cutback liquid asphalts are prepared by blending asphalt with a volatile solvent. The one of the following that is NOT used as an asphalt solvent is

    A. naphtha   B. gasoline   C. kerosene   D. toluene

    2.____

3. The primary purpose of the solvent in cutback asphalt is to allow the

    A. use of a larger size aggregate in the mix
    B. application of the asphalt at a relatively low temperature
    C. application of asphalt in wet weather
    D. application of asphalt in hot weather

    3.____

4. The thickness of the sheet asphalt on a sheet asphalt pavement is usually _____ inch(es).

    A. 1/2 inch to 3/4   B. 1 inch to 1 1/2
    C. 1 5/8 inches to 2   D. 2 1/4 inches to 3

    4.____

5. The grade of an asphalt cement is designated as AR4000.
   The AR is an abbreviation for

    A. asphalt rating   B. acid resistance
    C. aged residue   D. aging resistance

    5.____

6. An asphaltic emulsion is a suspension of asphalt in

    A. kerosene   B. gasoline   C. toluene   D. water

    6.____

7. A very light application of asphalt on an existing paved surface will promote bond between this surface and the subsequent course is known as a(n) _____ coat.

    A. prime   B. adhesion
    C. tack   D. penetrating

    7.____

8. Of the following, payment is usually made for asphalt pavements at the contract price per

    A. square inch   B. square foot
    C. square yard   D. 100 square feet

    8.____

9. The grade of an asphalt cement is designated AR4000. The 4000 is a measure of

   A. strength   B. viscosity   C. ductility   D. density

10. Of the following, the geometric shape of a horizontal curve on a highway is

    A. parabolic
    B. hyperbolic
    C. circular
    D. elliptical

11. A borrow pit in highway construction is used

    A. for storing stormwater in a heavy rain
    B. for coarse aggregate in Portland cement concrete
    C. for coarse aggregate in asphalt concrete
    D. to obtain fill for embankments

12. Overhaul in highway construction is usually measured and paid for by the

    A. yard - cubic foot
    B. yard - cubic yard
    C. station - cubic foot
    D. station - cubic yard

13. A Benkelman beam is used in highway work

    A. as an indicator of the ability of a pavement to withstand loading
    B. to measure the roughness of an asphalt concrete pavement
    C. to measure the uniformity of an asphalt concrete pavement
    D. to measure the ability of an asphalt concrete pavement to remain serviceable if the subgrade is undermined

14. When surfacing over an existing pavement, of the following, the MOST practical way to insure that the required thickness of new pavement is met is

    A. expansion of clay when exposed to water
    B. expansion of soil when excavated
    C. waviness in a soil embankment when being compacted with a roller
    D. expansion of loamy soil when exposed to water

15. When surfacing over an existing pavement, of the following, the MOST practical way to insure that the required thickness of new pavement is met is

    A. have wood blocks of the thickness of the new pavement temporarily placed on the existing pavement to insure that the thickness requirements will be met at the time of paving
    B. make a survey of the existing pavement elevations and a survey of the final pavement elevations and check that the thickness requirements are met
    C. check that the amount of asphalt delivered is adequate to meet the depth requirements of the area to be paved
    D. take core borings to determine if the thickness meets specifications

16. The maximum roller speed for steel tired rollers paving asphalt concrete is a maximum of _____ mile(s) per hour.

    A. 7   B. 5   C. 3   D. 1

17. The weathered or dry surface appearing on a relatively new pavement can generally be attributed to

    A. inadequate rolling
    B. oversized coarse aggregate in the mix
    C. excessive amount of fine aggregate
    D. insufficient asphalt in the mix

17._____

18. Construction contracts for highways have items paid either by unit price or lump sum. The one of the following that is usually a lump sum item on a highway contract is

    A. excavation   B. paving
    C. fencing   D. demolition

18._____

19. Highway roadway subgrades are usually required to have a relative density of _____ percent.

    A. 80 to 84   B. 85 to 89   C. 90 to 95   D. 100

19._____

20. A *profile* of a highway is

    A. the section taken along the centerline of the highway
    B. an aesthetic landscape sketch of the highway
    C. used to determine the line of the highway
    D. used to locate overpasses

20._____

21. A culvert as used under a highway is usually installed

    A. as a relief sewer
    B. as a bypass for a stream
    C. in a stream bed
    D. to carry sanitary and storm flow

21._____

22. A mass diagram as related to highway construction work is used to

    A. minimize traffic congestion
    B. compute payment for hauling excavation and fill
    C. find the largest feasible radius of curvature for a horizontal curve
    D. help determine the depth of an asphalt concrete pavement

22._____

23. The geometric shape of a vertical curve on a highway is a(n)

    A. parabola   B. hyperbola   C. circle   D. ellipse

23._____

24. When cast iron bell and spigot pipe is used in sewer construction, the joint is usually sealed with

    A. lead   B. tin
    C. cement mortar   D. oakum

24._____

25. A planimeter is used to measure

    A. location   B. area   C. elevation   D. angles

25._____

KEY (CORRECT ANSWERS)

1. C
2. D
3. B
4. B
5. C

6. D
7. C
8. B
9. B
10. C

11. D
12. D
13. A
14. B
15. A

16. C
17. D
18. D
19. C
20. A

21. C
22. B
23. A
24. A
25. B

TEST 2

DIRECTIONS: Each question or incomplete statement is followed by several suggested answers or completions. Select the one that BEST answers the question or completes the statement. *PRINT THE LETTER OF THE CORRECT ANSWER IN THE SPACE AT THE RIGHT.*

1. A witness stake is usually used in surveying primarily as   1._____

    A. proof that a given location has been surveyed
    B. an aid in locating a surveying stake
    C. a marker to prevent a stake being disturbed
    D. an offset stake

2. Before the contractor begins work on a sewer or highway project, a detailed survey is made of all existing structures that may be affected by the construction in order to   2._____

    A. protect against false claims for damage
    B. insure that the contractor causes no damage to property
    C. insure that existing elevations conform to elevations on the contract drawings
    D. uncover potential weaknesses in structures

3. The optimum moisture content of a given soil will result in the   3._____

    A. plastic limit of the soil is reached
    B. liquid limit of the soil is reached
    C. porosity of the soil is at its maximum
    D. soil is compacted to its maximum dry density

4. The letters SC for soil means   4._____

    A. silty clay   B. clayey sand
    C. sandy clay   D. clayey silt

5. A cradle is used under a large precast circular concrete pipe sewer. The purpose of the cradle is mainly to   5._____

    A. minimize the settlement of the earth on the sides of the sewer
    B. minimize the settlement under the pipe
    C. strengthen the pipe against collapse
    D. resist side pressure against the pipe

6. The joints on laid precast concrete pipe were poorly made.
The consequence of this poor workmanship is most likely   6._____

    A. the pipe will settle
    B. the pipe may collapse
    C. the water table may be adversely affected
    D. there will be excessive infiltration

7. An existing sewer is to connect into a new deep manhole for a new sewer. According to old plans for the existing sewer, the elevation of the existing sewer is 1/2 inch lower than shown on the plan.
Of the following, the BEST action that the inspector can take is   7._____

A. call his superior for instructions
B. do nothing
C. have the contractor relay the existing pipe to the theoretical elevation shown on the old plan
D. have an adjustable connection placed between the old pipe and the new manhole

8. The contractor proposes using a cement-lime mix for cement mortar to be used in building a manhole.
   This is

   A. *good* practice as this is a more workable mortar
   B. *good* practice as the mortar is slow setting
   C. *poor* practice because the mortar weakens in a wet environment
   D. *poor* practice as a cement-lime mortar is more porous than a cement mortar

9. Most serious claims for extra payment on large sewer contracts result from

   A. soil conditions that are markedly different from those that were presented by the owner
   B. the inspectors being unreasonable in their demands
   C. delay in making the areas available for work
   D. the fact that the method of construction required by the owner proved to be unworkable

10. Unconsolidated fill is at pipe laying depth. Of the following, the BEST action that an inspector can take is to

    A. have the unconsolidated fill removed and replaced with concrete
    B. have the unconsolidated fill removed and replaced with sound fill
    C. report this matter to your supervisor for his consideration
    D. ask the contractor to consolidate the fill

11. Buried debris not shown on the borings is uncovered near the surface of an excavation for a deep sewer. Of the following, the BEST action for an inspector to take is to

    A. record the depth and extent of the debris in the event of a claim
    B. do nothing as this has no effect on the final product
    C. notify the contractor that there is no valid claim for the extra work required
    D. be certain that the debris is not used in the backfill

12. A come-along or deadman is sometimes used in the laying of large precast concrete pipe to insure

    A. the pipe is at proper grade
    B. the pipe is on proper line
    C. that the pipe will not subsequently settle
    D. that the pipe is properly seated

13. In laying sewers,

    A. accuracy in the line of the sewer is more important than accuracy in the grade of the sewer
    B. accuracy in the grade of the sewer is more important than accuracy in the line of the sewer

C. accuracy in the line and grade of the sewer are equally important
D. since the sewer is underground, accuracy is not required either for line or grade

14. A sewer contract is given out with a price per foot of sewer for different diameter sewers. After the contract is let, the low bidder is required to give a breakdown of his price per foot of sewer to include excavation, sewer in place, backfill, and restoration. The purpose of this breakdown is to 14.___

   A. facilitate partial payments
   B. insure the bid is not unbalanced
   C. enable the agency to gather up-to-date cost data for future projects
   D. make it easier to price extra work

15. The house sewer runs from the house to the main line sewer. The size of this sewer is most frequently _____ inches. 15.___

   A. 4   B. 5   C. 6   D. 8

16. A line on centerline at the inside bottom of a pipe or conduit is known as the 16.___

   A. convert   B. invert   C. subvert   D. exvert

17. One of the most important elements of excavating for sewer construction is to maintain the specified width of the trench at the top of the pipe. If the width at the top of the pipe is too great, 17.___

   A. this may cause excessive settlement of the pipe
   B. this may cause excessive settlement of the backfill damaging the final pavement
   C. this may place excessive load on the pipe
   D. it may undermine utilities adjacent to the pipe

18. Wellpoints are used in sewer construction mainly to 18.___

   A. keep water out of the trench due to a heavy rainstorm
   B. keep water out of the excavation and subsoil to avoid excessive pressure on the sheeting
   C. prevent a boil from forming in the trench
   D. lower the water table to facilitate construction of the sewer

19. When a trench excavation uses soldier beams and horizontal sheeting for support, the minimum number of braces for each soldier beam is 19.___

   A. 1   B. 2   C. 3   D. 4

20. Bell and spigot pipe should be laid _____ with the bell end pointed _____. 20.___

   A. downstream; upstream   B. downstream; downstream
   C. upstream; upstream   D. upstream; downstream

21. The specifications state that house sewers should be laid at a grade of not less than 2%. In 40 feet of house sewer, the change in grade for 40 feet should be most nearly _____ inches. 21.___

   A. 8   B. 8 1/2   C. 9   D. 9 1/2

22. Two percent grade on a house sewer is equal to most nearly _____ inch per foot. 22.____

    A. 1/8 B. 3/16 C. 1/4 D. 5/16

23. When working underground in spaces that are closed and confined, such as manholes, the gas that is dangerous and most likely of the following to be present is 23.____

    A. carbon monoxide
    B. carbon dioxide
    C. ammonia
    D. methane

24. Of the following, air entrained cement would most likely be used in 24.____

    A. concrete roadways
    B. precast concrete pipe
    C. precast concrete manholes
    D. the cradle for precast concrete pipe

25. A slump cone is filled to overflowing in _____ layer(s). 25.____

    A. one
    B. two separate
    C. three separate
    D. four separate

KEY (CORRECT ANSWERS)

1.	B	11.	A
2.	A	12.	D
3.	D	13.	B
4.	B	14.	A
5.	B	15.	C
6.	D	16.	B
7.	B	17.	C
8.	C	18.	D
9.	A	19.	B
10.	C	20.	C

21. D
22. C
23. D
24. A
25. C

EXAMINATION SECTION
TEST 1

DIRECTIONS: Each question or incomplete statement is followed by several suggested answers or completions. Select the one that BEST answers the question or completes the statement. *PRINT THE LETTER OF THE CORRECT ANSWER IN THE SPACE AT THE RIGHT.*

1. In pouring concrete for a large footing, the vibrator is used to move concrete into place. This is

   A. *good* practice as it moves the concrete quickly into place
   B. *good* practice as it eliminates air pockets
   C. *poor* practice as it promotes segregation
   D. *poor* practice as it increases pressure against the forms

   1.____

2. For successful winter work in placing ordinary concrete, adequate protection against the cold should be provided.
   Special protection is NOT required when the temperature is over _____ and is required when the temperature is below _____.

   A. 50° F; 50° F
   B. 40° F; 40° F
   C. 30° F; 30° F
   D. 20° F; 20° F

   2.____

3. The MAIN reason for curing concrete is to

   A. prevent segregation of the concrete
   B. prevent the formation of air pockets in the concrete
   C. keep the concrete surface moist
   D. minimize bleeding in the poured concrete

   3.____

4. Of the following, the concrete mix that uses the greatest amount of cement per cubic yard of concrete is

   A. 1:2:4   B. 1:2:3 1/2   C. 1:2 1/2:5   D. 1:2 1/2:3 1/2

   4.____

5. The volume of concrete in a sidewalk 6 ft. x 30 ft. x 4 inches is, in cubic feet, MOST NEARLY

   A. 45   B. 50   C. 55   D. 60

   5.____

6. Of the following, the chemical compound that is added to a concrete mix to accelerate setting in cold weather is

   A. potassium chloride
   B. calcium chloride
   C. sodium nitrate
   D. calcium nitrate

   6.____

7. The compressive strength of concrete

   A. reaches a maximum after 28 days
   B. reaches a maximum after 90 days
   C. reaches a maximum after 180 days
   D. increases after 180 days

   7.____

8. The smallest size of coarse aggregate for concrete is, in inches, MOST NEARLY

   A. 1/4   B. 3/8   C. 1/2   D. 5/8

8.____

9. Of the following, the most practical way to determine that the water used in a concrete mix is satisfactory is

   A. send a sample to the laboratory
   B. taste the water
   C. the water is also used for drinking
   D. take a sample and let it stand for a while; and if no sediment at the bottom of the sample, it is satisfactory

9.____

10. Grout is

    A. cement, sand with water added so that it will flow readily
    B. cement with water added so that it is fluid
    C. cement and lime with water added so that it will flow readily
    D. gravel, sand, and lime with water added so that it will flow readily

10.____

11. Wire fabric has a designation 4 x 12 6/10. Of the following, the statement that is correct is the _____ center to enter and are _____.

    A. longitudinal wires are 12"; 10 gage
    B. longitudinal wires are 4"; 6 gage
    C. transverse wires are 4"; 6 gage
    D. transverse wires are 12; 6 gage

11.____

12. The volume of a bag of cement is _____ cubic foot(feet).

    A. 1   B. 1 1/2   C. 2   D. 2 1/2

12.____

13. The specifications state: *Forms for slabs shall be set with a camber of 1/4 inch for each 10 feet of span.* The purpose of this requirement is to

    A. compensate for deflection
    B. allow for small errors in setting the formwork
    C. allow for shrinkage of the concrete
    D. compensate for settlement of the supports for the formwork

13.____

14. When an inspector goes out to inspect the reinforcing steel before placing of the concrete, the most important drawings he should have with him are the _____ drawings.

    A. structural steel   B. reinforcing steel detail
    C. formwork   D. erection

14.____

15. A reinforcing bar has hooks at each end as shown at the right. The detail drawing of the bar will show dimension

    A. A
    B. B
    C. C
    D. D

15.____

16. Concrete sidewalks are usually finished with a

    A. screed
    B. steel float
    C. wood float
    D. darby

17. A new manhole consists of a concrete base made with ordinary cement and a brick superstructure. The minimum time that is usually required after the pouring of the concrete base to start the brickwork is _____ hours.

    A. 24   B. 48   C. 72   D. 96

18. In a new manhole, the slump in the concrete used in the base should be _____ inches.

    A. 2 to 3   B. 3 to 4   C. 4 to 5   D. 5 to 6

19. The dimensions of a cylinder used for testing the strength of concrete is _____ inch diameter and _____ inches high.

    A. 6; 9   B. 6; 12   C. 8; 9   D. 8; 12

20. The specification for the mixing time required for a concrete mix in a Ready-Mix truck is one minute for a one cubic yard batch and a quarter of a minute for every additional cubic yard. The minimum mixing time for a ten cubic yard batch is _____ minutes.

    A. 2 3/4   B. 3   C. 3 1/4   D. 3 1/2

21. The subgrade for a concrete footing is wetted down before concrete is poured into the footing.
    This is

    A. *poor* practice as the water-cement ratio of the concrete will be increased
    B. *poor* practice as it will leave a pocket on the underside of the footing
    C. *good* practice as the water-cement ratio of the concrete will be decreased
    D. *good* practice as the soil will not withdraw water from the concrete

22. Concrete should not be poured too rapidly into the formwork for thin walls primarily because

    A. segregation will result
    B. air pockets will form in the wall
    C. there will be excessive pressure on the formwork
    D. there will be seepage of water through the formwork.

23. The FIRST step in finishing the surface of a concrete pavement is

    A. darbying   B. floating   C. screeding   D. tamping

24. The grade of a reinforcing steel is 40. The 40 represents the _____ of the steel.

    A. tensile strength
    B. ultimate strength
    C. yield point
    D. elastic limit

25. In reinforced concrete work, stirrups would MOST likely be found in

    A. beams   B. columns   C. walls   D. footings

KEY (CORRECT ANSWERS)

1.	C	11.	B
2.	B	12.	A
3.	C	13.	A
4.	B	14.	B
5.	D	15.	D
6.	B	16.	C
7.	D	17.	A
8.	B	18.	A
9.	C	19.	B
10.	A	20.	C

21. D
22. C
23. C
24. C
25. A

TEST 2

DIRECTIONS: Each question or incomplete statement is followed by several suggested answers or completions. Select the one that BEST answers the question or completes the statement. *PRINT THE LETTER OF THE CORRECT ANSWER IN THE SPACE AT THE RIGHT.*

Questions 1-6.

DIRECTIONS: Questions 1 through 6, inclusive, refer to the following retaining wall.

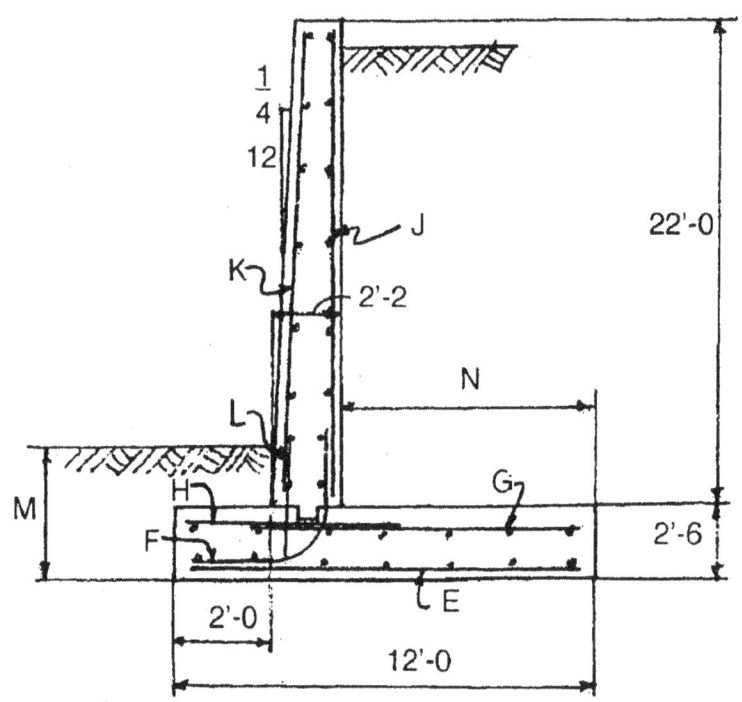

1. The largest size steel bars are most likely to be   1.___
   A. H, K, L   B. E, F, J   C. F, G, H   D. F, G, J

2. Distance M is USUALLY at least   2.___
   A. 2'6"   B. 3'0"   C. 3'6"   D. 4'0"

3. Dimension N is   3.___
   A. 7'6"   B. 7'8"   C. 7'10"   D. 8'0"

4. The width of the wall at the top of the wall is   4.___
   A. 1'8"   B. 1'8 1/2"   C. 1'9"   D. 1'9 1/2"

5. The volume of one foot of wall, in cubic feet, is most nearly (neglect the key at the bottom of the wall)   5.___
   A. 41.2   B. 41.7   C. 42.2   D. 42.6

6. The number of cubic yards of concrete in the footing fifty feet long is, in cubic yards, most nearly (neglect the key at the bottom of the wall)

   A. 54.6   B. 55.6   C. 56.6   D. 57.6

6._____

Questions 7-9.

DIRECTIONS: Questions 7 through 9, inclusive, refer to the markings on a reinforcing bar. The end of a reinforcing bar is marked H6N60.

7. The H in H6N60 indicates the

   A. method of treatment of the reinforcing bar
   B. hardness of the reinforcing steel bar
   C. initial of the steel mill
   D. type of steel in the reinforcing bar

7._____

8. The N in the reinforcing steel bar means

   A. new billet steel
   B. normalized reinforcing steel
   C. the area in which the steel has been produced (north east)
   D. the initial of the manufacturer

8._____

9. The 60 represents the

   A. ultimate strength of the steel
   B. diameter of the steel in millimeters
   C. allowable unit stress in the steel
   D. grade of the steel

9._____

10. The plywood industry produces a special product intended for concrete forming called

    A. structure ply   B. plyform
    C. formply   D. plycoat

10._____

11. Lumber that has been inspected and sorted will carry a grade stamp. The item LEAST likely to be found on the grade stamp is

    A. state of origin   B. grade
    C. species   D. condition of seasoning

11._____

12. In dimensioned lumber, wane indicates

    A. a lack of lumber
    B. narrow annular rings
    C. undersized width or length of lumber
    D. improper seasoning

12._____

13. A sidewalk slab is required to be 4" thick. Measuring down from a nail in the side form that represents the top of the slab, the distance is 4 1/2 inches. Of the following, the BEST action to take is

    A. have the contractor fill the subgrade with a half inch of sand
    B. have the contractor fill the subgrade with a half inch of grout

13._____

C. take no action as the contract requirement is met
D. point out the discrepancy to the contractor and ask him to take appropriate action

14. If high visibility is necessary on the job, a vest _____ colored should be worn. 14._____

    A. red   B. orange   C. yellow   D. green

15. Emulsified asphalt tack coats are preferred to using cut back asphalts PRIMARILY because 15._____

    A. cut-back asphalts present environmental problems
    B. cut-back asphalts are slower drying than emulsified asphalts
    C. cut-back asphalts are faster drying than emulsified asphalts
    D. emulsified asphalts are easier to place than cut-back asphalts

16. Spread footings are footings that 16._____

    A. cover a large area
    B. have an irregular shape
    C. are sometimes called strap footings
    D. transmit their loads through a combination of piles and soil

17. An excavation for a footing is over-excavated and the subgrade is well below the design elevation. Of the following, the BEST action for the contractor to take is 17._____

    A. fill the excavation with well compacted soil until it reaches the design elevation of the bottom of the footing
    B. fill the subgrade with gravel to reach the bottom elevation of the footing
    C. lower the elevation of the footing but retain its thickness
    D. change the footing to a pile supported footing

18. The inspector should be aware of the items in the contract that are unit price so that he can 18._____

    A. make the proper inspection of these items
    B. keep a record of when they are delivered to the job site
    C. make measurements and compute quantities that may be necessary
    D. record the dates of installation of these items

19. The attitudes that an inspector should adopt in dealing with the contractor are to be 19._____

    A. understanding and flexible
    B. helpful and cautious
    C. cautious and skeptical
    D. firm and fair

20. Among the provisions for the safety of workers on the job, the most basic and general one is 20._____

    A. workmen should work slowly
    B. keep alcohol off the job
    C. good housekeeping
    D. wear suitable clothing for extreme weather conditions

21. Ladders should extend a minimum of _____ above the level to which they lead.   21._____

    A. six feet
    B. knee-high
    C. waist-high
    D. five feet

22. An inspector notices a worker working in an unsafe manner. Of the following, the BEST action the inspector can take is to   22._____

    A. tell the worker the correct way to work
    B. tell the worker's supervisor of the unsafe behavior of the worker
    C. record the incident in your log book
    D. notify the contractor so that the unsafe practice will cease

23. In making the daily report, personal remarks by the inspector should not be included. Of the following, the best reason for this exclusion is   23._____

    A. it may raise questions as to the accuracy of the report
    B. the wrong people may read the daily report
    C. the inspector should have no opinions
    D. it may indicate bias on the part of the inspector

24. The major difference between a softwood and a hardwood in forestry terms is   24._____

    A. the softwoods are from the south and the hardwoods are from the north
    B. the softwoods are evergreens and the hardwoods are deciduous
    C. the softwoods are soft and the hardwoods are hard
    D. there is one grading method for softwoods and another grading method for hardwoods

25. Lumber is considered unseasoned if it has a moisture content of not less than _____ percent in weight of water.   25._____

    A. 17
    B. 20
    C. 23
    D. 26

KEY (CORRECT ANSWERS)

1.	D	11.	A
2.	D	12.	A
3.	C	13.	C
4.	B	14.	B
5.	D	15.	A
6.	B	16.	A
7.	C	17.	A
8.	A	18.	C
9.	D	19.	D
10.	B	20.	C

21. C
22. B
23. D
24. B
25. B

EXAMINATION SECTION
TEST 1

DIRECTIONS: Each question or incomplete statement is followed by several suggested answers or completions. Select the one that BEST answers the question or completes the statement. *PRINT THE LETTER OF THE CORRECT ANSWER IN THE SPACE AT THE RIGHT.*

1. An unbalanced bid is a bidding device used by the contractor. An example of unbalanced bidding is to put

    A. lower unit prices in all unit price items to submit a low bid
    B. lower prices on lump sum items and higher prices on unit price items
    C. lower unit prices on secondary items and higher unit prices on primary items
    D. higher prices on items built early and lower prices on items built later

2. Clearing and grubbing as related to excavation mean cutting trees

    A. so that 1 foot remains above ground
    B. so that 6 inches remains above ground
    C. to ground level
    D. and removing the stumps of the trees

3. The size of a bulldozer is measured by its

    A. weight
    B. flywheel horsepower
    C. ripping capacity
    D. coefficient of traction

4. Of the following, an important use of geotextiles is

    A. as a filter in drainage control
    B. to improve the density of soil
    C. to increase the plasticity of soil
    D. to reduce the CBR of soil

5. A graphical procedure employing a control chart is sometimes used for statistical control in highway construction. After charts of individual tests are prepared, the upper and lower limits are usually _____ standard deviation(s) from a central value.

    A. one   B. two   C. three   D. four

6. On a highway construction job, slope stakes are usually set on both sides of the road at intervals of _____ feet.

    A. 25   B. 50   C. 75   D. 100

7. Earth grade stakes are usually set

    A. when the slope stakes are set
    B. at the center line of the road
    C. after final grading is completed
    D. after rough grading operations have been completed

8. In a borrow pit, measurements for the volume of earth removed are taken usually at _____ foot intervals.

   A. 25 B. 50 C. 75 D. 100

9. In placing surveying stakes for a culvert, a stake is set at the center line of the culvert. A horizontal line on the stake gives the amount of cut or fill to the _____ of the culvert.

   A. top B. center C. flow line D. subgrade

10. Aeolian soils are soils formed by

    A. glacial action
    B. volcanic action
    C. being carried by water
    D. being carried by wind

11. Specific gravity of soils are in the range of

    A. 2.3 to 2.5
    B. 2.4 to 2.6
    C. 2.5 to 2.7
    D. 2.6 to 2.8

12. Of the following soils, the one that is most highly compressible has a _____ plastic limit and _____ liquid limit.

    A. low; high
    B. low; low
    C. high; low
    D. high; high

13. In the present ASSHTO soil classification systems, soils are classified into groups. The number of basic groups are

    A. 6 B. 7 C. 8 D. 9

14. In the present AASHTO soil classification system, granular materials are primarily in Group(s)

    A. A1 *only*
    B. A1 and A2
    C. A1, A2, and A3
    D. A1, A2, A3, and A4

15. The optimum moisture content of a soil occurs when under a given compactive effort, the soil has a maximum

    A. void ratio
    B. plasticity index
    C. elasticity
    D. density

16. The liquid limit that separates an A4 soil from an A5 soil is

    A. 10 B. 20 C. 30 D. 40

17. As part of the soil classification in a given soil is an abbreviation NP. This is an abbreviation for no

    A. permeability
    B. plasticity
    C. peat or other organic materials
    D. porosity

18. For granular materials, the maximum allowable percent passing a Number 200 sieve is

    A. 20 B. 25 C. 30 D. 35

19.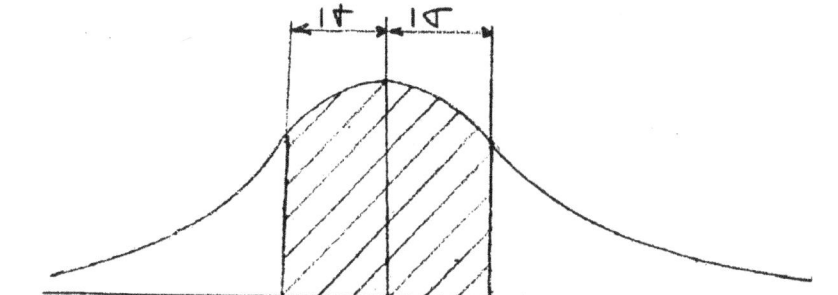

In the normal or Gauss distribution shown above, the shaded area is one standard deviation on either side of the central value covering _____ of the area under the curve.

A. 60% B. 62% C. 65% D. 68%

Questions 20-25.

DIRECTIONS: Questions 20 through 25, inclusive, refer to the diagram below of a vertical curve.

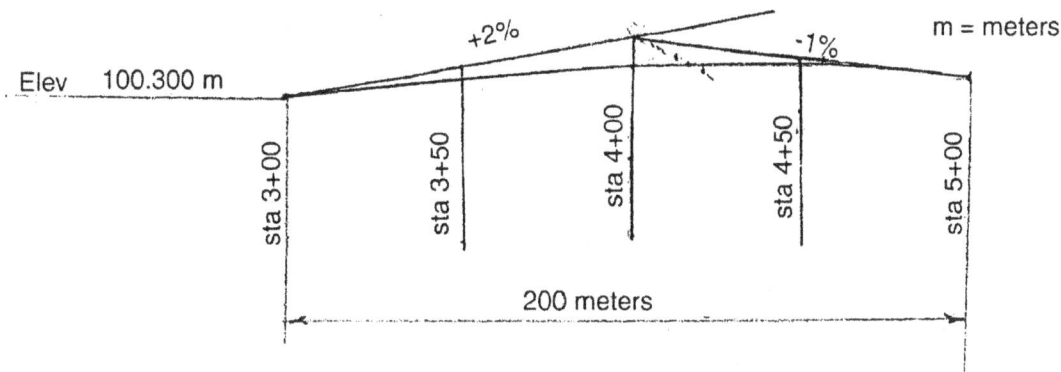

20. The elevation of the curve at Sta4+00 is _____ meters.

    A. 101.250 B. 101.350 C. 101.850 D. 102.150

21. The grade of the curve at Sta4+00 is

    A. +.5% B. +.75% C. +1.00% D. +1.25%

22. The elevation of the curve at Sta3+50 is _____ meters.

    A. 100.992 B. 101.012 C. 101.112 D. 101.212

23. The grade of the curve at Sta3+50 is

    A. 1.75% B. 1.50% C. 1.38% D. 1.25%

24. The station of the high point is

    A. 4+08.333 B. 4+16.667 C. 4+25.000 D. 4+33.333

25. The elevation of the high point is _____ meters.

    A. 101.633 B. 101.750 C. 101.833 D. 101.917

KEY (CORRECT ANSWERS)

1.	D	11.	D
2.	D	12.	A
3.	B	13.	B
4.	A	14.	C
5.	C	15.	D
6.	B	16.	D
7.	D	17.	B
8.	A	18.	D
9.	C	19.	D
10.	D	20.	B

21. A
22. C
23. D
24. D
25. A

TEST 2

DIRECTIONS: Each question or incomplete statement is followed by several suggested answers or completions. Select the one that BEST answers the question or completes the statement. *PRINT THE LETTER OF THE CORRECT ANSWER IN THE SPACE AT THE RIGHT.*

Questions 1-3.

DIRECTIONS: Questions 1 through 3 refer to the diagram below.

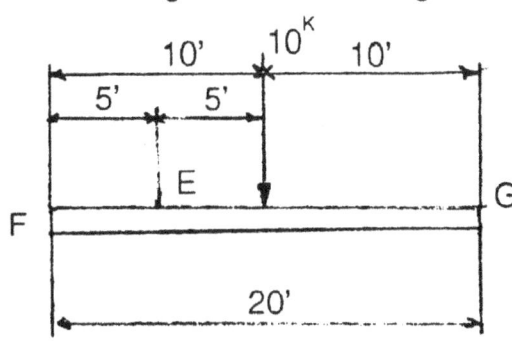

EI is constant

1. The deflection at the center of the beam is

   A. $-\dfrac{1670^{k^{13}}}{EI}$ B. $-\dfrac{2000^{k^{13}}}{EI}$ C. $-\dfrac{2330^{k^{13}}}{EI}$ D. $-\dfrac{2670^{k^{13}}}{EI}$

   1.____

2. The slope at F is

   A. $-\dfrac{200^{k^{12}}}{EI}$ B. $-\dfrac{225^{k^{12}}}{EI}$ C. $-\dfrac{250^{k^{12}}}{EI}$ D. $-\dfrac{275^{k^{12}}}{EI}$

   2.____

3. The deflection at E is

   A. $-\dfrac{966^{k^{13}}}{EI}$ B. $-\dfrac{1046^{k^{13}}}{EI}$ C. $-\dfrac{1096^{k^{13}}}{EI}$ D. $-\dfrac{1146^{k^{13}}}{EI}$

   3.____

Questions 4-7.

DIRECTIONS: Questions 4 through 7, inclusive, refer to the truss below.

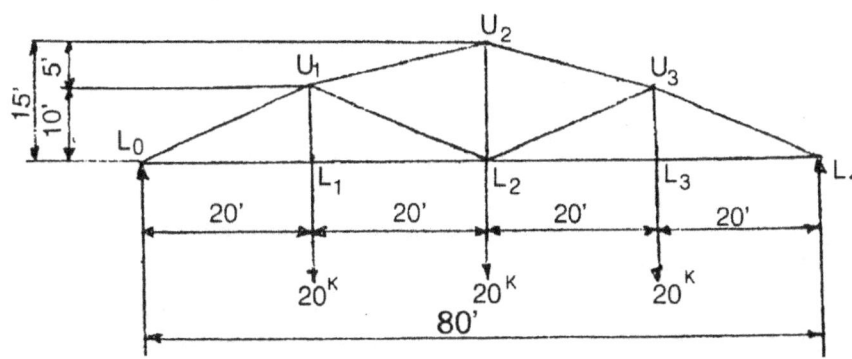

4. The load in member L_1-L_2 is 4.____

   A. $+30^k$ B. $+40^k$ C. $+50^k$ D. $+60^k$

5. The load in member U_1-U_2 is 5.____

   A. -50.9^k B. -52.9^k C. -54.9^k D. -56.9^k

6. The load in member U_1-L_2 is 6.____

   A. -3.4^k B. -5.4^k C. -7.4^k D. -9.4^k

7. The load in member U_2-L_2 is 7.____

   A. $+24.6^k$ B. $+26.6^k$ C. $+28.6^k$ D. $+30.6^k$

Questions 8-11.

DIRECTIONS: Questions 8 through 11, inclusive, refer to the diagram below of a beam with fixed ends.

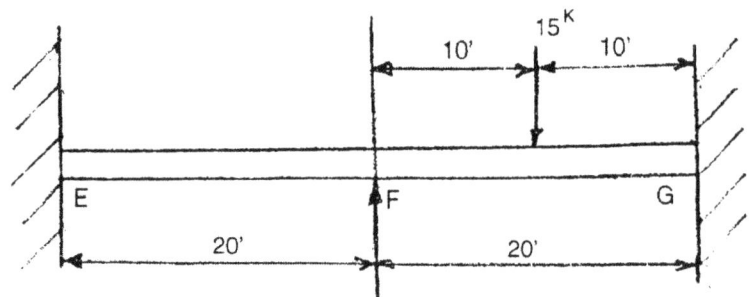

8. The moment in E is 8.____

   A. 9.4^{lk} B. 12.6^{lk} C. 14.8^{lk} D. 17.0^{lk}

9. The moment in G is 9.____

   A. 37.5^{lk} B. 40.0^{lk} C. 43.0^{lk} D. 46.9^{lk}

10. The moment at F is 10.____

    A. 14.4^{lk} B. 18.8^{lk} C. 23.2^{lk} D. 27.6^{lk}

11. The vertical reaction at E is 11.____

    A. -0.4^k B. -1.4^k C. -2.4^k D. -3.4^k

12. The former First Lady of the United States who had legislation enacted to plant wild flowers adjacent to federal highways is 12.____

    A. Rosalyn Carter B. Barbara Bush
    C. Jackie Kennedy D. Lady Bird Johnson

13. *Scarification* as used in the specifications means 13.____

    A. removing rust from a surface
    B. removing paint from a surface
    C. cleaning equipment
    D. loosening topsoil

14. A proposal by the contractor producing a savings to the department without impairing essential functions and characteristics of the facility is termed a(n) 14.____

    A. alternative suggestion
    B. design efficiency proposal
    C. value engineering proposal
    D. force account economy

15. A cubic meter is MOST NEARLY equal to _____ cubic yards. 15.____

    A. 1.31   B. 1.33   C. 1.35   D. 1.37

16. One hectare is equal to MOST NEARLY _____ acres. 16.____

    A. 2   B. 2.5   C. 3.0   D. 3.5

17. One newton is MOST NEARLY equal to _____ pounds. 17.____

    A. .12   B. .17   C. .22   D. .29

18. A metric ton is _____ pounds. 18.____

    A. 2200   B. 2400   C. 2600   D. 2800

19. A piezometer is a device that measures 19.____

    A. hydraulic pressure   B. soil compaction
    C. soil grain size   D. soil grain strength

20. Portland cement type 2 is _____ cement. 20.____

    A. high early strength
    B. low heat
    C. air entraining
    D. moderate sulfate resisting

21. Wire shall have a minimum yield strength of 240 MPa. The MPa is an abbreviation of _____ pascals. 21.____

    A. macro   B. micro   C. milli   D. mega

22. 7°C is, in degrees Fahrenheit, 22.____

    A. 42.6   B. 44.6   C. 46.6   D. 48.6

23. In a concrete mix, the absolute ratio of the weight of water to the weight of cement is .44. If a bag of cement weighs 94 pounds and there are 7.48 gallons in a cubic foot, the number of gallons of water per bag of cement for this ratio is MOST NEARLY 23.____

    A. 5.0   B. 5.5   C. 5.8   D. 6.1

24. The specifications require that when transit mixed concrete is used, approximately 90% of the design water is added followed by mixing the concrete in the drum of the truck. The remainder of the design water may be added

    A. after half the load is emptied
    B. to meet the water cement ratio requirement
    C. if the mix is not uniform
    D. to attain a suitable slump

25. For highways, the minimum median width in a divided highway is _____ feet.
    A. 2   B. 3   C. 4   D. 5

KEY (CORRECT ANSWERS)

1. A
2. C
3. D
4. D
5. C
6. C
7. B
8. A
9. D
10. B
11. B
12. D
13. D
14. C
15. A
16. B
17. C
18. A
19. A
20. D
21. D
22. B
23. A
24. D
25. C

EXAMINATION SECTION
TEST 1

DIRECTIONS: Each question or incomplete statement is followed by several suggested answers or completions. Select the one that BEST answers the question or completes the statement. *PRINT THE LETTER OF THE CORRECT ANSWER IN THE SPACE AT THE RIGHT.*

Questions 1-2.

DIRECTIONS: Questions 1 and 2 refer to the formula below.

The formula for stopping sight distance SSD13

$$SSD = 1.47tV + \frac{V^2}{30(f+G)}$$

1. The number 1.47 is a(n)

   A. empirically derived constant
   B. conversion factor
   C. factor based on perception reaction time
   D. factor of safety

2. The term t is usually assumed to be _____ seconds.

   A. 1.5   B. 2.0   C. 2.5   D. 3.0

3. An automobile weighing W is rounding a curve of radius R with a velocity V. Neglecting the friction between the tires and the roadway, if the forces acting on the car are in equilibrium, then

A. $\sin\theta = \dfrac{V^2}{gR}$

B. $\cos\theta = \dfrac{V^2}{gR}$

C. $\tan\theta = \dfrac{V^2}{gR}$

D. $\cot\theta = \dfrac{V^2}{gR}$

Questions 4-5.

DIRECTIONS: Questions 4 and 5 refer to the horizontal curve below.

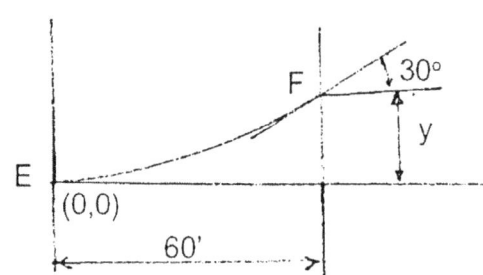

The equation of the curve is $y = kx^3$. The slope of the curve at F is 30°.

4. The value of k is
   A. .000023   B. .000033   C. .000043   D. .000053

5. The value of y is
   A. 5.0   B. 7.1   C. 9.3   D. 11.5

6. A 4° horizontal curve has a radius of _____ feet.
   A. 1232.4   B. 1332.4   C. 1432.4   D. 1532.4

Questions 7-10.

DIRECTIONS: Questions 7 through 10, inclusive, refer to the diagram of a horizontal circular highway curve.

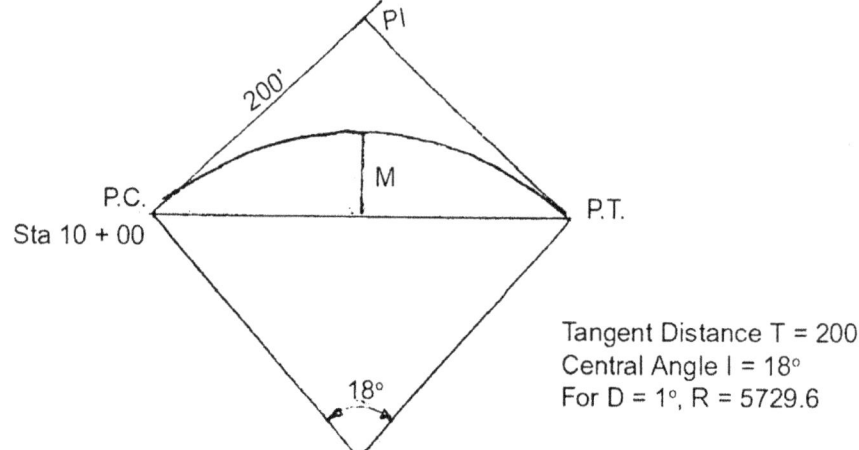

Tangent Distance T = 200'
Central Angle I = 18°
For D = 1°, R = 5729.6

7. The radius of the curve is _____ feet.
   A. 1212.7   B. 1232.7   C. 1262.7   D. 1292.7

8. The length of the arc of the circular curve is MOST NEARLY _____ feet.
   A. 396.7   B. 397.0   C. 397.7   D. 398.0

9. The long chord P.C. to P.T. is MOST NEARLY _____ feet.

   A. 392.06   B. 393.06   C. 394.06   D. 395.06

10. The middle ordinate M is most nearly _____ feet.

    A. 14.95   B. 15.15   C. 15.35   D. 15.55

11.

The sight distance EF is MOST NEARLY _____ feet.

   A. 324   B. 364   C. 404   D. 444

12. For crest vertical curves, the length of the curve depends on the change in grade and H_e and H_o where He is the driver's eye height and H_o is the object height. Their relation is usually

    A. $H_e < H_o$
    B. $H_e = H_o$
    C. $H_e > H_o$
    D. H_e is either greater, equal or less than H_o, depending on the judgment of chief of design

13. The length of a transition curve which connects a tangent to a circular curve should be sufficient to

    A. keep the rate of change of direction small
    B. achieve the superelevation of the road section
    C. prevent disruption of the drainage system
    D. prevent an abrupt change of direction when the circular curve is reached

14. It is desirable to have a minimum road grade of at least 0.3% in order to

    A. follow the land contours
    B. facilitate keeping the shoulders clear of debris
    C. secure adequate drainage for the roadway
    D. prevent drivers becoming drowsy on long stretches of level roadway

Questions 15-16.

DIRECTIONS: Questions 15 and 16 refer to the horizontal highway curve below.

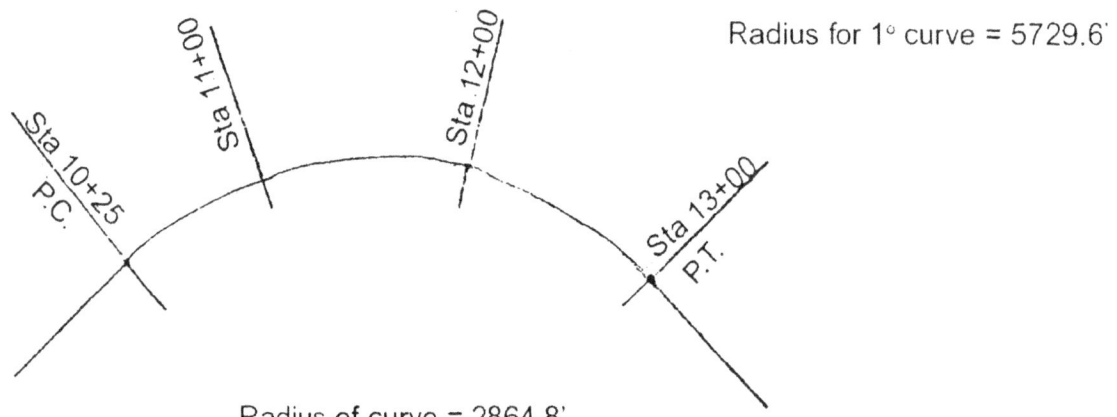

Radius for 1° curve = 5729.6'

Radius of curve = 2864.8'

15. The deflection angle from the P.C. to Sta 11+00 is

    A. 0°45'   B. 1°00'   C. 1°15'   D. 1°30'

16. The deflection angle to Sta 13+00 is

    A. 2°00'   B. 2°45'   C. 3°45'   D. 5°30'

17. Air entrained cement is used in air entrained concrete. The acceptable amount of air is generally between _____ percent of the total volume.

    A. 1 and 5   B. 2 and 6   C. 3 and 7   D. 4 and 8

18. Pumping of joints in a concrete roadway slab will occur during frequent occurrence of heavy wheel loads, the presence in the subgrade soil that is susceptible to pumping and

    A. inadequate thickness of the concrete slab
    B. air entrained cement is used in the roadway
    C. surplus water in the subgrade
    D. coarse and fine sand subgrades

19. Distributed steel reinforcing is primarily used to control cracking of a concrete roadway pavement and to maintain the integrity of the slab between transverse joints. Wire fabric or bar mats are used.
    In a concrete roadway section, the steel is usually placed at _____ of the slab.

    A. or near the center
    B. the bottom
    C. the top
    D. the bottom and at the top

20. In slipform paving for a concrete roadway, the slump in the concrete being poured should be _____ inch(es).

    A. 1/2 to 1   B. 1 to 1 1/2   C. 1 1/2 to 2   D. 2 to 2 1/2

21. The collapse of a section of the New England Thruway at Mianus was due primarily to faulty   21._____

    A. steel
    B. design
    C. construction
    D. periodic inspections

22. The coefficient of expansion of concrete due to temperature change is considered   22._____

    A. the same as that for steel
    B. less than that for steel
    C. more than that for steel
    D. more or less than that for steel, depending on the type of steel being used

23. Design hourly volume is a future hourly volume used for design. It is usually taken as the _____ hourly volume of the year.   23._____

    A. 10th   B. 15th   C. 20th   D. 30th

24. Let E be an experiment and S a sample space associated with the experiment. A function X assigned to every element SES a real number X(S) is called a   24._____

    A. relative frequency
    B. likely outcome
    C. random variable
    D. conditional probability

25. The color code brown on a traffic device denotes   25._____

    A. public recreation and scenic guidance
    B. construction and maintenance warning
    C. general warning
    D. motorist service guidance

KEY (CORRECT ANSWERS)

1. B		11. D	
2. C		12. C	
3. C		13. B	
4. D		14. C	
5. D		15. A	
6. C		16. B	
7. C		17. D	
8. A		18. C	
9. D		19. A	
10. D		20. B	

21. D
22. A
23. D
24. C
25. A

TEST 2

DIRECTIONS: Each question or incomplete statement is followed by several suggested answers or completions. Select the one that BEST answers the question or completes the statement. *PRINT THE LETTER OF THE CORRECT ANSWER IN THE SPACE AT THE RIGHT.*

1. The minimum headroom clearance for a sign over a roadway, according to the Federal Highway Administration, should be _____ feet.

   A. 15 B. 16 C. 17 D. 18

2. In traffic flow, time mean speed _____ space mean speed.

   A. equals
   B. is less than
   C. is greater than
   D. may be greater or less than

3. Overall speed and running speed are speeds over a relatively long section of street or highway between an origin and a destination. Test vehicles are driven over the test section of the roadway. The driver attempts to float in the traffic stream.
   This means

   A. driving as fast as he can under the speed limit
   B. driving in the middle lane of a three lane road
   C. passing as many vehicles as pass the test vehicle
   D. trying to keep his speed the same as the average speed of the vehicles on the road

4. The difference between overall speed and running speed on a test run between origin and destination is overall speed is the

   A. average of the maximum and minimum speed while running speed is the distance covered divided by the time elapsed
   B. distance traveled divided by the time required while running speed is the distance traveled divided by the time required reduced by time for stop delays
   C. distance traveled divided by the total time required while running speed is the minimum time needed to cover the distance
   D. distance traveled divided by the total time required while running speed is the effort by the driver to stay in the flow of traffic

5. The ductility test on asphalt is considered a measure of the _____ of the asphalt.

   A. impact resistance   B. elasticity
   C. durability   D. cementing power

6. In asphalt paving work, there are three different types of specific gravity: bulk, apparent, and effective. Of the following statements relating to specific gravity, the one that is CORRECT is:

   A. Water absorption is normally not used in determining the quantity of permeable voids in the volume of aggregates
   B. The apparent specific gravity is less than the bulk specific gravity

C. The effective specific gravity is less than the bulk specific gravity
D. The effective specific gravity falls between the bulk specific gravity and the apparent specific gravity

7. The temperature range of asphalt prior to entering the mixer in a batch or continuous plant is usually

   A. 150 to 250° F
   B. 175 to 275° F
   C. 200 to 300° F
   D. 225 to 325° F

8. The most likely cause of the various distress types in asphalt concrete pavements is

   A. structural failure
   B. temperature changes
   C. moisture changes
   D. faulty construction

9. Bleeding in asphalt concrete pavements is MOST likely caused by

   A. faulty mix composition
   B. structural failure
   C. temperature changes
   D. moisture changes

10. Depressions in asphalt concrete pavements is MOST likely caused by

    A. faulty construction
    B. faulty mix composition
    C. temperature changes
    D. moisture changes

11. The gradation curve of particle sizes is represented graphically with the ordinate defining the percent by weight passing a given size and the abscissa representing the particle size.
    The ordinate is plotted on a(n) _____ scale and the abscissa is plotted on a(n) _____ scale.

    A. arithmetic; arithmetic
    B. logarithmic; arithmetic
    C. arithmetic; logarithmic
    D. logarithmic; logarithmic

12. The viscosity of a liquid is a measure of its

    A. resistance to flow
    B. volatility
    C. solubility in carbon tetrachloride
    D. elasticity

13. Failures that occur in soil masses as a result of the action of highway loads are primarily _____ failures.

    A. tensile   B. torsion   C. shear   D. buckling

14. Bitumens composed primarily of high molecular weight hydrocarbons are soluble in

    A. toluene
    B. carbon sulfate
    C. carbon disulfide
    D. ammonium chloride

15. One pascal-second equals _____ poise(s).

    A. 1   B. 5   C. 10   D. 20

16. RS emulsions are best used

    A. where deep penetration is desired
    B. with coarse aggregates
    C. in warm weather
    D. in spraying applications

17. The specific gravity of bituminous material is generally determined

    A. with a pyenometer
    B. with a hygrometer
    C. by displacement
    D. with a hydrometer

18. The principal reason for determining the specific gravity of a bituminous material is

    A. converting from volume to weight measurements and vice versa
    B. identifying the type of bituminous material used in a mix
    C. for checking the uniformity of a mix where large quantities are involved
    D. insure that the properties of the mix continue to meet specifications

19. The specific gravity of asphaltic products derived from petroleum vary from

    A. .80 to .84
    B. .92 to 1.06
    C. 1.04 to 1.18
    D. 1.16 to 1.30

20. The flash point is an indirect measurement of the quality and kind of volatiles present in the asphalt being tested.
    Rapid cure cutback asphalts have a flashpoint of _____ or less.

    A. 100° F
    B. 130° F
    C. 150° F
    D. 180° F

21. Traffic density is defined as the

    A. number of vehicles passing a given point in a given period of time
    B. average number of vehicles occupying a given length of roadway at a given instant
    C. average center to center distance of vehicles on a given stretch of roadway at a given instant
    D. minimum distance center to center of vehicles on a given stretch of roadway at a given instant

22. Of the following, the best distribution that describes the vehicle distribution on a given stretch of highway at a given instant is the _____ distribution.

    A. Poisson
    B. Pascal
    C. normal
    D. hypergeometric

23. In slipform paving for a concrete roadway, the slump in the concrete being poured should be _____ inch(es).

    A. 1/2 to 1
    B. 1 to 1 1/2
    C. 1 1/2 to 2
    D. 2 to 2 1/2

24. A water-cement ratio of 6 gallons per sack of cement is equal to a water-cement ratio of _____ by weight.

    A. .50
    B. .53
    C. .56
    D. .59

25. One micron is equal to _____ centimeters. 25._____

  A. 10^{-2} B. 10^{-3} C. 10^{-4} D. 10^{-5}

KEY (CORRECT ANSWERS)

1. C
2. C
3. C
4. B
5. D

6. D
7. D
8. D
9. A
10. A

11. C
12. A
13. C
14. C
15. C

16. D
17. A
18. A
19. B
20. A

21. B
22. A
23. B
24. B
25. C

EXAMINATION SECTION
TEST 1

DIRECTIONS: Each question or incomplete statement is followed by several suggested answers or completions. Select the one that BEST answers the question or completes the statement. *PRINT THE LETTER OF THE CORRECT ANSWER IN THE SPACE AT THE RIGHT.*

1. In the future there will be a push for all transportation infrastructure to achieve *sustainable development*. An example of *sustainable development* is

    A. increase the number of lanes on a highway to accommodate added traffic
    B. decrease the number of deaths per million miles of automobile traffic
    C. recycle components of the infrastructure to minimize use of nonrenewable resources
    D. reduce the cost of constructing a mile of highway

    1.____

2. Pressures are mounting to adopt planning and the principles of TQM. TQM is the abbreviation for

    A. Transportation Quality Management
    B. Transportation Quality Maintenance
    C. Total Quality Management
    D. Total Quality Maintenance

    2.____

3. Ladybird Johnson's contribution to highways was

    A. the planting of wildflowers adjacent to the highway
    B. the planting of trees along the highways
    C. beautifying highway exits with trees and flowers
    D. improving safety at highway exits

    3.____

4. Bituminous materials used for highways include asphalts and tars derived from destructive distillation of materials such as coal and wood. Tars have been little used recently primarily because of

    A. high cost of the tar
    B. inability to meet the specifications for tar
    C. difficulty in applying this material
    D. lack of availability of the material

    4.____

5. Contraction joints in a Portland cement concrete highway slab are provided in order to

    A. allow the slab to crack at the joint
    B. minimize hydroplaning in wet weather
    C. absorb expansion of the slab
    D. control alligator cracks on the surface of the slab

    5.____

6. Of the following, the one that is designated as a grade of asphalt binder is

    A. AD   B. AS   C. PR   D. PG

    6.____

7. A property of asphaltic materials is viscosity. Viscosity in a liquid is the

   A. resistance to evaporation
   B. tendency to separate into its components
   C. ability of the liquid to mix with other materials
   D. tendency of the liquid to resist flow

8. Medium-curing cutback asphalt contains a _____-type solvent.

   A. kerosene   B. naphtha
   C. heavy fuel oil   D. benzene

9. Asphalt emulsions are becoming the preferred asphalt binder in many agencies because

   A. emulsions are easier to apply
   B. of concern about hydrocarbon emissions from cut-back asphalts
   C. emulsions produce an asphalt concrete that is more resistant to abrasion
   D. emulsions are more resistant to water penetration

10. An example of vector control on a roadside is

    A. eliminating a breeding ground for rodent populations
    B. keeping signs and directions in good condition
    C. keeping the roadside free of litter and debris
    D. halting erosion on the roadside

11. An attenuator in highway work is a(n)

    A. warning device during highway maintenance work
    B. barrier to protect highway maintenance workers
    C. overhead warning to slow down automobiles
    D. crash safety board

12. Preventive maintenance is a planned strategy of cost effective treatment that preserves the system.
    It can BEST be expressed as

    A. don't fix it if it isn't broken
    B. a stitch in time saves nine
    C. if something can go wrong it will
    D. it is preferable to replace than repair

13. There are two types of aggregate used in asphalt mixes: crushed aggregate and round aggregate. Of the following statements relating to the two types of aggregate, the one that is CORRECT is:

    A. There is no advantage in either aggregate.
    B. Round aggregate is preferable to crushed aggregate.
    C. Crushed aggregate is preferable to round aggregate.
    D. It all depends on the source of the aggregate.

14. Temperature limits should be strictly observed when using asphalt cements. The mixing temperature should be between

   A. 125° F and 175° F
   B. 175° F and 225° F
   C. 275° F and 325° F
   D. 325° F and 375° F

15. When high early strength is desired in Portland cement concrete, the cement to use is type

   A. II B. III C. IV D. V

16. The main purpose of grading aggregates in an asphalt roadway mix is to

   A. provide a good surface
   B. provide a strong mix
   C. minimize the quantity of asphalt required
   D. provide a dense mix to prevent water seepage in the roadway

17. The wearing quality of an aggregate is determined by testing for resistance to

   A. abrasion
   B. crushing
   C. chemical deterioration
   D. frost

18. According to the AASHTO Maintenance Manual on Roadways, earth-aggregate roadway surfaces and subsurfaces are most effective when they have achieved at least _____% of their compaction capacity.

   A. 80 B. 85 C. 90 D. 95

19. Superelevation on a highway usually occurs

   A. on an approach to a bridge
   B. on a horizontal highway curve
   C. at a high point on a vertical highway curve
   D. at a low point on a vertical highway curve

20. Shoulders have two basic purposes in the roadway system: they provide lanes for emergency or safe travel and they

   A. prevent vegetation encroaching on the roadway surface
   B. allow seepage into the subgrade of runoff from the roadway surface
   C. provide room for barriers
   D. provide lateral support to the pavement structure

21. For roadway cross-sections without curbs, shoulder cross slopes usually range from _____ for paved surfaces.

   A. 1% to 3% B. 3% to 5% C. 5% to 7% D. 7% to 9%

22. If turf shoulders are used on a roadway, the advantage of using native grasses usually is that native grasses

   A. do not need mowing
   B. are more pleasing to the eye than imported grasses
   C. are less-expensive than other grasses
   D. do not need irrigation

23. A deep rut in an aggregate shoulder at the edge of a hard-surfaced roadway can usually be corrected by reshaping the shoulder MOST efficiently with a

    A. scarifier
    B. bulldozer
    C. motor grader
    D. roller

23.____

24. A method of scheduling shoulder maintenance in response to risk management efforts is to

    A. maximize the life of the shoulder
    B. minimize the labor cost of maintaining the shoulder in a serviceable condition
    C. defend maintenance policies and practices in the event of accident litigation involving the shoulders
    D. use a database to predict when maintenance and repair will be required for the shoulders

24.____

25. Spalling of the surface of a concrete roadway is generally caused by

    A. inadequate vibrating when pouring the concrete
    B. too low a water/cement ratio in the concrete mix
    C. expansion of the concrete
    D. the use of epoxy-coated reinforcing bars in the concrete

25.____

KEY (CORRECT ANSWERS)

1.	C	11.	D
2.	C	12.	B
3.	A	13.	C
4.	D	14.	C
5.	A	15.	B
6.	D	16.	C
7.	D	17.	A
8.	A	18.	D
9.	B	19.	B
10.	A	20.	D

21.	B
22.	D
23.	C
24.	C
25.	C

TEST 2

DIRECTIONS: Each question or incomplete statement is followed by several suggested answers or completions. Select the one that BEST answers the question or completes the statement. *PRINT THE LETTER OF THE CORRECT ANSWER IN THE SPACE AT THE RIGHT.*

1. Corrosion of reinforcing bars in a reinforced concrete road pavement can be caused by water entering the concrete road pavement or _____ entering the concrete road pavement.

    A. sulfates   B. chlorides   C. carbonates   D. fluorides

2. A tack coat applied to an old roadway surface creating a bond between the old and the new surface is applied with a distributor at the rate of _____ gallon per square yard.

    A. .05 to .15   B. .15 to .25
    C. .25 to .35   D. .35 to .45

3. Some voids should be included in compacted asphaltic concrete to allow for expansion in hot weather. Surface course voids is usually recommended to be

    A. 2% to 4%   B. 4% to 6%   C. 6% to 8%   D. 8% to 10%

4. The highest temperature that asphalts can withstand is

    A. 300° F   B. 350° F   C. 400° F   D. 450° F

5. A polymer is a substance containing

    A. microscopic air bubbles
    B. the element silicon
    C. a definite lattice arrangement
    D. giant molecules

6. The one of the following that is not a polymer concrete is _____ concrete.

    A. epoxy   B. methyl methacrylate
    C. polyurethane   D. vermiculite

7. It is suspected that a given stretch of existing roadway may have substructure problems; that is, the soil under the roadway is weak.
   Of the following, the BEST method of testing the sub-surface is with a _____ test.

    A. falling weight deflectometer
    B. soil porosity
    C. consolidation settlement
    D. tiltmeter

8. The one of the following that is NOT a claimed potential advantage of using reclaimed asphalt paving for a new asphalt pavement is

    A. energy saving
    B. cost reduction
    C. stronger asphalt pavement
    D. conservation of natural resources

9. Mineral dust is added to asphalt primarily to _____ asphalt.

   A. make it easier to roll the
   B. increase the viscosity of the
   C. stabilize the
   D. eliminate air pockets in

10. The smallest size sieve that mineral dust should pass through is No.

    A. 50   B. 100   C. 150   D. 200

11. Most asphalt used in highway construction is derived from

    A. natural sources
    B. coal distillation
    C. inorganic materials
    D. petroleum distillation

12. Asphalt emulsions should be cationic or anionic depending on

    A. the pH value of the asphalt
    B. aggregate size distribution
    C. the pH value of the water used
    D. the type of aggregates used

13. Air-entrained cement is used in concrete to

    A. expose concrete to severe frost action
    B. give the concrete high early strength
    C. resist sulfate deterioration
    D. make the concrete more workable

14. The main purpose of vibrating poured concrete is to

    A. eliminate air pockets in the placed concrete
    B. prevent segregation in the concrete
    C. allow excess water to rise to the surface
    D. decrease the water/cement ratio in the poured concrete

15. The primary purpose of curing a concrete road slab shortly after pouring is primarily to

    A. prevent loss of water in the concrete due to evaporation
    B. protect the concrete from changes in outside temperature
    C. shield the surface of the concrete against the loss of heat
    D. prevent segregation in the concrete slab

16. A bag of Portland cement weighs MOST NEARLY _____ pounds.

    A. 82   B. 86   C. 90   D. 94

17. The water/cement ratio for 4,000 pounds per square inch concrete is, in gallons of water per bag of concrete, MOST NEARLY

    A. 3   B. 5   C. 7   D. 9

Questions 18-19.

DIRECTIONS: Questions 18 and 19 refer to the notes shown below.

The notes shown below are used to determine the elevation of the top of a manhole M.

Point	BS	HI	F.S.	Elevation
BMA	0.72			151.42'
Manhole M			4.25	

18. The elevation of manhole M is, in feet and inches, MOST NEARLY 18.____

    A. 140.45   B. 148.95   C. 153.89   D. 162.39

19. The elevation of manhole M, in feet and inches, is MOST NEARLY 19.____

    A. 148'-5 3/8" B. 148'-11 3/8"
    C. 153'-10 11/16" D. 162'-4 11/16"

20.

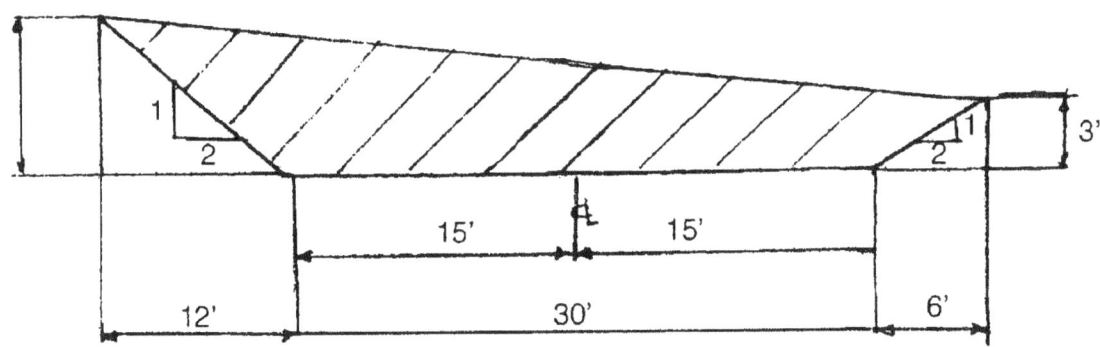

The cross-section area of the excavation shown above is, in square feet, MOST NEARLY
A. 171   B. 175   C. 179   D. 183

21. The cross-section area of the sewer section is, in square feet, MOST NEARLY 21.____

    A. 12.2
    B. 12.4
    C. 12.6
    D. 12.8

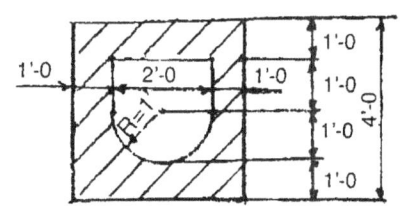

22. 3.66 meters is MOST NEARLY _____ feet. 22.____

    A. 11   B. 12   C. 13   D. 14

23. In some states litigation has established a legal definition of a safety hazard as any pavement dropoff exceeding 5.1 centimeters. This, in inches, is MOST NEARLY 23.____

    A. 1   B. $1\frac{1}{2}$ C. 2   D. $2\frac{1}{2}$

24. In a roadway maintenance manual is a subject heading titled AESTHETIC OBJEC- 24.____
TIVES. An example of an aesthetic objective is to

    A. reduce highway accidents
    B. enhance a roadway's scenic qualities
    C. improve the roadway's drainage system
    D. widen the roadway at a turnout to prevent vehicles backing up into the highway

25. A cubic yard of ordinary unreinforced concrete weighs MOST NEARLY _____ pounds. 25.____

    A. 2000   B. 3000   C. 4000   D. 5000

KEY (CORRECT ANSWERS)

1.	B	11.	D
2.	A	12.	D
3.	B	13.	A
4.	D	14.	A
5.	D	15.	A
6.	D	16.	D
7.	A	17.	B
8.	C	18.	C
9.	C	19.	C
10.	D	20.	A

21. B
22. B
23. C
24. B
25. C

EXAMINATION SECTION
TEST 1

DIRECTIONS: Each question or incomplete statement is followed by several suggested answers or completions. Select the one that BEST answers the question or completes the statement. *PRINT THE LETTER OF THE CORRECT ANSWER IN THE SPACE AT THE RIGHT.*

1. Reinforcing steel is coated with epoxy primarily to _____ of the steel. 1.___

   A. prevent corrosion
   B. improve the electric conductivity
   C. increase the tensile strength
   D. increase the compressive strength

2. Specifications for concrete require that concrete shall reach or exceed the design strength at the end of days. 2.___

   A. 14   B. 21   C. 28   D. 35

3. A #G reinforcing bar has a cross-section area of square inches. 3.___

   A. .44   B. .48   C. .52   D. .56

4. Mixing time for concrete which is measured from the time all ingredients are in the drum should be at least 1.5 minutes for a one cubic yard mixer plus 0.5 minutes for each cubic yard of capacity over one cubic yard.
   The MINIMUM time to mix 7 cubic yards of concrete is, in minutes, 4.___

   A. 3.0   B. 3.5   C. 4.0   D. 4.5

5. It is recommended that a maximum limit be set on mixing time for machine-mixed concrete because overmixing may remove entrained air and 5.___

   A. increase the water/cement ratio of the mixture
   B. increase the amount of fine aggregates in the concrete mixture
   C. the concrete mix may set prematurely
   D. cause excess water to rise in the placed concrete causing alligator cracks in the surface

6. 6.___

   Of the following curves, the shape of the roadway section shown above is

   A. circular   B. elliptical   C. parabolic   D. hyperbolic

7.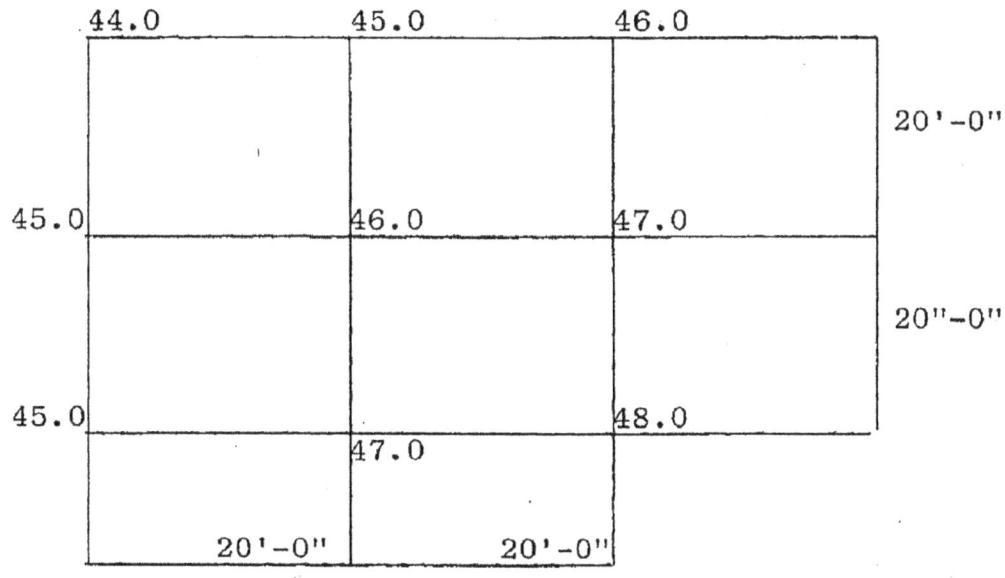

Shown above are the elevations of a borrow pit. The final elevation of the borrow pit after removing the soil is 40.0. Neglecting earth removal outside the borrow pit area, the volume of earth removed is, in cubic yards, MOST NEARLY
A. 347   B. 352   C. 357   D. 362

8. The shaded area is, in square inches, MOST NEARLY
   A. 18.3
   B. 19.1
   C. 20.0
   D. 20.9

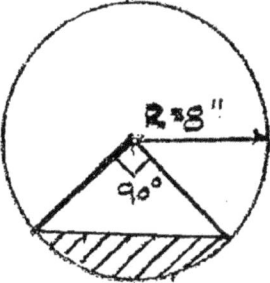

9. Of the following properties of polymer concrete that make it attractive for maintenance of Portland cement concrete roadways, the one that is MOST important is

   A. light weight
   B. immunity to corrosion
   C. resistance to abrasion
   D. rapid hardening qualities

10. A gallon of water weighs MOST NEARLY _____ pounds.

    A. 7.53   B. 8.33   C. 9.13   D. 9.53

11. Air-entrained concrete is used in concrete roadways primarily to

    A. reduce the weight of the concrete
    B. prevent corrosion of the steel reinforcement in the concrete
    C. make the concrete less porous to the intrusion of water in the concrete
    D. resist damage to the roadway due to freezing and thawing

12. The slump test in concrete is used to test its

    A. air content B. workability
    C. porosity D. uniformity

13. The criterion for water that is to be used for mixing concrete is that it should be potable. This means that the water should

    A. have high turbidity
    B. should be hard
    C. contain no sulfates
    D. be fit for human consumption

14. A test that can be used on an asphalt roadway to measure changes in hardness due to age hardening is a _____ test.

    A. ductility
    B. viscosity
    C. ring and ball softening point
    D. penetration

15. A densely graded bituminous mixture is called a large stone mix if the nominal size of aggregates is equal to or greater than a minimum of

    A. 1 inch B. 1 1/4 inches
    C. 1 1/2 inches D. 1 3/4 inches

16. The specifications state that the surface on which the bituminous material is applied must have a temperature of 20°C or higher.
    20°C is, in degrees Fahrenheit,

    A. 62° B. 64° C. 66° D. 68°

17. The largest size aggregate in sheet asphalt is usually

    A. 1/8 inch B. 1/4 inch C. 3/8 inch D. 1/2 inch

18. Sheet asphalt is used mainly in

    A. rural areas B. major highways
    C. overpasses D. city streets

19. Of the following, a slurry seal is NOT used on a bituminous pavement to

    A. fill potholes
    B. fill cracks
    C. repair raveling asphalt pavement
    D. provide a skid-resistant surface

20. Pozzolan is a *siliceous* material. Another example of a siliceous material is

    A. clay B. limestone C. granite D. sand

21. The primary purpose of a tack coat that precedes the application of a bitumimous mix on an existing surface is to

    A. remove dust from the existing surface
    B. fill in cracks in the existing surface
    C. allow the new mixture to adhere to the existing surface
    D. prevent the asphalt in the bituminous paving material from seeping into the existing pavement

22. The lowest temperature at which asphalt pavements should be laid is

    A. 30°F B. 40°F C. 50°F D. 60°F?

23. Steam will rise from an asphalt mix when it is dumped into the hopper of a paver if

    A. there is too little asphalt in the mix
    B. excess moisture is present in the mix
    C. the mix is too hot
    D. there is an excess of asphalt in the mix

24. The number of millimeters in an inch is MOST NEARLY

    A. 20 B. 25 C. 30 D. 35

25. The number of inches in a meter is MOST NEARLY

    A. 39.37 B. 39.57 C. 39.77 D. 39.97

KEY (CORRECT ANSWERS)

1. A
2. C
3. A
4. D
5. B
6. C
7. B
8. A
9. D
10. B
11. D
12. B
13. D
14. D
15. A
16. D
17. B
18. D
19. A
20. D
21. C
22. B
23. B
24. B
25. A

TEST 2

DIRECTIONS: Each question or incomplete statement is followed by several suggested answers or completions. Select the one that BEST answers the question or completes the statement. *PRINT THE LETTER OF THE CORRECT ANSWER IN THE SPACE AT THE RIGHT.*

1. Overheated asphalt can often be identified from the _____ in the truck.   1._____
   A. rich black appearance and the tendency to slump
   B. slump and leveling out
   C. blue smoke rising from the mix
   D. lean, granular appearance of the mix

2. Of the following, the traffic sign shown at the right indicates a   2._____
   A. school crossing
   B. no passing zone
   C. railroad crossing
   D. deer crossing

3. 90 kilometers per hour is MOST NEARLY _____ miles per hour.   3._____
   A. 40   B. 45   C. 50   D. 55

4. One kilometer is equal to _____ miles.   4._____
   A. 0.5   B. 0.6   C. 0.7   D. 0.8

5. Steel weighs 490 pounds per cubic foot. A one inch square bar of steel one foot long weighs MOST NEARLY _____ pounds.   5._____
   A. 3.0   B. 3.4   C. 3.8   D. 4.2

6. The size of the fillet weld is dimension   6._____
   A. A
   B. B
   C. C
   D. D

   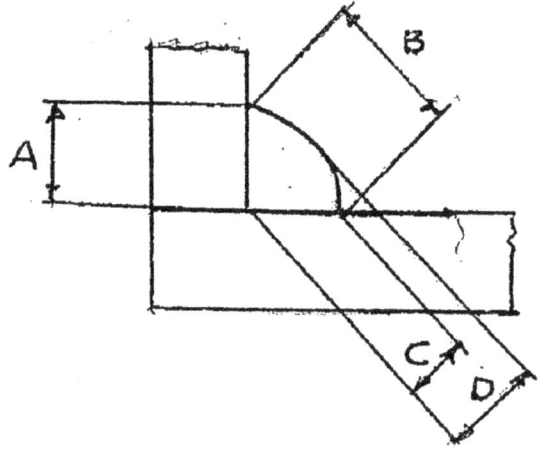

7. In mowing planted and natural grass adjacent to a roadway, the preferable period is   7._____
   A. winter   B. spring   C. summer   D. fall

8. Pumping of a roadway surface occurs on

   A. bituminous pavements only
   B. bituminous and concrete pavements
   C. concrete pavements only
   D. concrete pavements only if they are not air-entrained

9. Pumping of a roadway surface is associated with soils in the subgrade that are

   A. gravelly
   B. fine grained
   C. coarse grained
   D. distributed in size from fine grained soils to coarse grained soils

10. The buckling or blowup of old concrete pavements is due primarily to the

    A. failure of longitudinal and transverse joints to function properly
    B. pounding by trucks that the pavement was not designed to carry
    C. failure of the subgrade to transfer the loads upon it
    D. subsurface water that is not drained from beneath the pavement

11. The MOST common type of construction equipment used for clearing and grubbing activities is a bulldozer. Bulldozer size is determined by

    A. tread area   B. blade size
    C. drawbar pull   D. flywheel horsepower

12. Sheepsfoot rollers are BEST used to compact

    A. clay soils   B. sandy soils
    C. gravelly soils   D. graded sand and gravel mix

13. A smooth-wheeled steel roller that is typically water ballasted are most effective on

    A. granular material such as sand and gravel
    B. clayed material
    C. mixtures of silt, sand and clay
    D. mixtures of sand and clay

14. Of the following machines, the one that would be MOST suitable for grading and shaping surfaces, ditching and bank sloping would be a

    A. bulldozer   B. motor grader
    C. front end loader   D. backhoe

15. Supercompactors which are useful for all types of soils weigh from _____ tons.

    A. 10 to 40   B. 20 to 50   C. 30 to 60   D. 40 to 70

16. A basic objective of the Critical Path Method used on a highway construction project would be to

    A. achieve economies in the use of material
    B. achieve economies in the use of equipment
    C. improve the quality of construction
    D. prevent the creation of bottlenecks

17. In the Critical Path Method, free float is the amount of time   17.___

    A. an activity requires to be completed
    B. an activity can be delayed without causing a delay in the succeeding activity
    C. an activity takes to make up for the time lag in the following activity
    D. needed to make up for lost time in a preceding activity

18. Another name for the bar chart used in construction planning and scheduling is the   18.___
    _____ chart.

    A. Fischer   B. Schiff   C. Banff   D. Gantt

19. Of the following, the machine that would LEAST likely be used to excavate large volumes   19.___
    of earth is a

    A. scraper   B. front end loader
    C. shovel   D. clamshell

20. Roadside maintenance generally includes the area between the   20.___

    A. traveled surface and the limits of the right of way
    B. distance between the outer edges of the shoulders on opposite sides of the highway
    C. median strip of the highway
    D. distance between the right of way on opposite sides of the highway

21. The sewer that usually has the greatest depth below grade is usually a(n)_____ sewer.   21.___

    A. sanitary   B. combined
    C. intercepting   D. relieving

22. A combined sewer is a sewer that   22.___

    A. carries storm water and salty water
    B. is made of steel and lined on the inside with concrete
    C. sometimes flow less than full and sometimes is under pressure
    D. carries sewage and storm water

23. If the grade of a sewer is 0.5%, the change in the elevation of the invert of the sewer in   23.___
    350 feet is, in feet and inches,

    A. 1'-9"   B. 1'-10"   C. 1'-11"   D. 2'-0"

24. The National Joint Committee has adopted a color code for traffic control devices. The   24.___
    color brown is used for

    A. direction guidance
    B. general warning
    C. motorist service guidance
    D. public recreation and scenic guidance

25. Of the following, the isosceles traffic sign shown at the right indicates a
    A. traffic separation
    B. no U turn
    C. narrow median-urban
    D. no passing zone

25.____

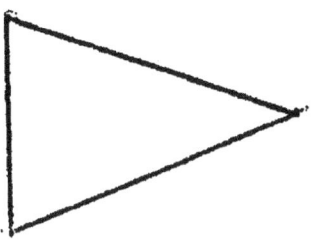

KEY (CORRECT ANSWERS)

1. C
2. A
3. D
4. B
5. B

6. A
7. D
8. C
9. B
10. A

11. D
12. A
13. A
14. B
15. B

16. D
17. B
18. D
19. D
20. A

21. C
22. D
23. A
24. D
25. D

EXAMINATION SECTION
TEST 1

DIRECTIONS: Each question or incomplete statement is followed by several suggested answers or completions. Select the one that BEST answers the question or completes the statement. *PRINT THE LETTER OF THE CORRECT ANSWER IN THE SPACE AT THE RIGHT.*

1. The specifications denote the ultimate strength of concrete at the end of _____ days.   1._____
   A. 7   B. 14   C. 21   D. 28

2. The one of the following that is NOT a purpose of adding an admixture to the concrete mixture is   2._____
   A. set retardation
   B. water reduction
   C. required air content
   D. increase hardness

3. When a highway slab is to be placed by slipform paving, it is essential that the concrete mix have a   3._____
   A. large slump
   B. small slump
   C. high air content
   D. low air content

4. Of the following, the accepted method used to insure that the thickness of a sidewalk slab meets the specified minimum depth is to   4._____
   A. have the contractor certify that it meets the specified required depth
   B. measure the depth of the slab at its edge
   C. take a core boring of the slab
   D. place a test load on a square foot of the slab to insure the slab has an adequate bearing capacity

5. Calcium chloride is sometimes added to a concrete mix as a(n) _____ agent.   5._____
   A. retarding
   B. air entraining
   C. curing
   D. accelerating

6. *Pumping* in a highway concrete slab refers to the   6._____
   A. ejection of water and soil along the edges of a concrete slab
   B. raising of a concrete highway slab due to frost heave
   C. bulging of a concrete slab when high temperature causes excessive expansion of a slab at an expansion joint
   D. raising and falling of a concrete slab caused by a rise in the water table

7. The material used in madjacking consists primarily of _____ sand, cement and water.   7._____
   A. gypsum, coarse
   B. coarse
   C. gypsum, fine
   D. fine

8. A gallon of water weighs _____ pounds per cubic foot.   8._____
   A. 8.00   B. 8.15   C. 8.33   D. 8.45

9. Of the following, the one that would NOT be used as a dust palliative on a road surface would be

   A. calcium sulfate
   B. calcium chloride
   C. sodium chloride
   D. bituminous substances

10. One of the items in highway maintenance is *soil sterilants*. The primary purpose of soil sterilants is to

   A. prevent the spread of mosquitos
   B. prevent the growth of weeds
   C. discourage wild animals from using the road
   D. encourage the growth of wild flowers

Questions 11-16.

DIRECTION: Questions 11 through 16, inclusive, refer to the following chart describing the gradation of a subbase for a highway pavement.

Sieve Size Designation	Percent Passing By Weight
75mm	100
50mm	90-100
6.3mm	30-65
425µmm	5-40
75µmm	0-10

11. The maximum percent that can be retained on the 50mm screen is

   A. 0   B. 5   C. 10   D. 15

12. The maximum percent that can be retained on the 6.3mm screen is

   A. 40   B. 50   C. 60   D. 70

13. The minimum percent that must be retained on the 6.3mm screen is

   A. 20   B. 25   C. 30   D. 60

14. The maximum size of aggregate for the subbase is MOST NEARLY _____ inches.

   A. 2   B. 2 1/2   C. 3   D. 3 1/2

15. µmm is equal to a _____ of a meter.

   A. thousandth
   B. ten-thousandth
   C. hundred thousandth
   D. millionth

16. µ in the metric system is a prefix for

   A. milli   B. micro   C. nano   D. pico

17. The specifications state that sodium chloride shall be packed in moisture-proof bags not containing more than 45 kg each.
    The MAXIMUM weight per bag, in pounds, is

   A. 95   B. 97   C. 99   D. 101

18. In placing corrugated steel pipe with longitudinal seams, the longitudinal seams shall be placed   18.____

    A. at the sides of the pipe
    B. at the top of the pipe
    C. at the bottom of the pipe
    D. wherever it is convenient for the contractor

19. In placing corrugated steel pipe, the circumferential seams with laps shall be placed with   19.____

    A. one lap facing upstream and the next lap facing downstream
    B. laps facing in the downstream direction
    C. laps facing in the upstream direction
    D. laps lap welded to the adjacent pipe

20. Before laying corrugated steel pipe, the specifications require that the contractor shall provide the inspector equipment to measure the gauge of the pipe.   20.____
    The equipment referred to is a

    A. micrometer
    B. steel rule that measures to a 64th of an inch
    C. manometer
    D. caliper

21. The thickness of the galvanized coating on a corrugated steel pipe can be measured with a(n)   21.____

    A. fixed probe magnetic gauge
    B. ultrasonic probe
    C. laser gauge
    D. piezometer

22. Terne plate is steel plate coated with   22.____

    A. zinc   B. lead   C. copper   D. tin

23. The cross-section area of a No. 9 reinforcing steel bar is _____ square inches.   23.____

    A. .60   B. .875   C. 1.00   D. 1.128

24. The weight per foot of a No. 9 reinforcing bar is MOST NEARLY _____ pounds per foot.   24.____

    A. 1.8   B. 2.04   C. 3.4   D. 3.64

25. The diameter of a No. 9 bar is _____ inch(es).   25.____

    A. 0.75   B. 0.875   C. 1   D. 1.125

KEY (CORRECT ANSWERS)

1. D
2. D
3. B
4. C
5. D

6. A
7. D
8. C
9. A
10. B

11. C
12. D
13. B
14. C
15. D

16. B
17. C
18. A
19. B
20. D

21. A
22. D
23. C
24. C
25. D

TEST 2

DIRECTIONS: Each question or incomplete statement is followed by several suggested answers or completions. Select the one that BEST answers the question or completes the statement. *PRINT THE LETTER OF THE CORRECT ANSWER IN THE SPACE AT THE RIGHT.*

1. A reinforcing steel bar is designated Grade 40. The 40 refers to its   1.____

    A. allowable working stress
    B. yield point
    C. elastic limit
    D. ultimate strength

2. The epoxy coating of a reinforcing bar is tested by bending the bar 120 about a mandrel of specified diameter. This test is defined as a(n) _____ test.   2.____

    A. adhesion   B. tensile   C. shear   D. bearing

3. The hourly rate of flow of sewage is not constant but varies between _____ percent of the daily average.   3.____

    A. 90 to 110   B. 70 to 130   C. 50 to 150   D. 30 to 170

4. If the slope of a sewer pipe is .003. The change in elevation in 100 feet is   4.____

    A. 3 1/2"   B. 3 5/8"   C. 3 3/4"   D. 4"

5. The minimum allowable velocities in sanitary sewers is _____ feet per second.   5.____

    A. 1 to 1.5   B. 1.5 to 2   C. 2.0 to 2.5   D. 2.5 to 3.0

6. Catch basins are designed to   6.____

    A. slow down the flow of storm water
    B. filter out organic material from the storm water
    C. clean grit before it enters the storm sewer
    D. catch grit admitted through street inlets and prevent it from entering the storm water drains

7. Before workmen go into a manhole to do repair work, it is necessary to suck out the air from the manhole and replace it with fresh air. The MAIN purpose of replacing the air in the sewer manhole is to remove   7.____

    A. methane gas   B. carbon dioxide
    C. carbon disulfide   D. hydrogen disulfide

8. Sewage consists primarily of fresh water and has less than _____ percent of solid matter.   8.____

    A. 0.1   B. 0.2   C. 0.3   D. 0.4

9. Fresh sewage has only a slight odor, but when stale it becomes septic and has a strong _____ odor.   9.____

    A. vinegary   B. sweetish
    C. benzene   D. hydrogen sulfxde

70

Questions 10-11.

DIRECTIONS: Questions 10 and 11 refer to the section of an existing concrete sewer.

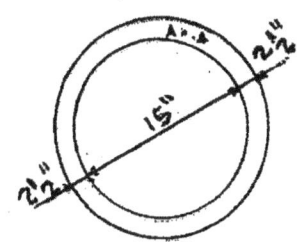

10. If the elevation of the top of the sewer is 24,572 feet, the elevation of the invert of the sewer is ———— feet.

    A. 23.114   B. 23.052   C. 22.965   D. 22.905

11. The cross-section area of the concrete section is sq.in.

    A. 131.5   B. 133.5   C. 135.5   D. 137.5

12. The reason for using wellpoints in the construction of sewers is usually to

    A. prevent the formation of boils
    B. lower the water table
    C. overcome the existence of quicksand
    D. keep the trench dry in the event of a rainstorm

13. Shown at the right is a sewer section with a concrete cradle. The area of the cradle is ____ square feet.
    A. 1.60
    B. 1.66
    C. 1.72
    D. 1.78

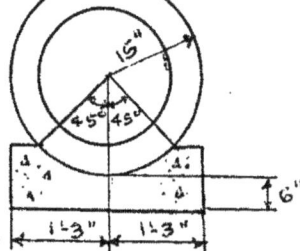

14.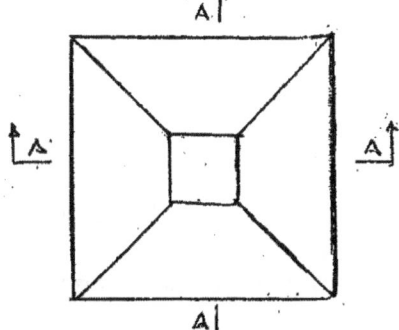

Plan

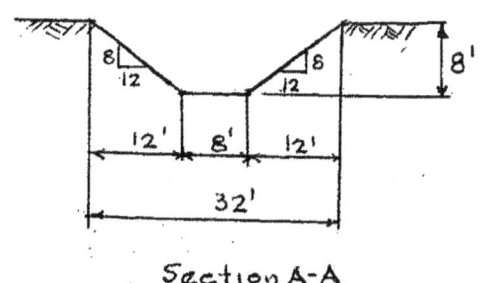

Section A-A

The volume of excavation by the prismoidal formula is _____ cubic yards.

A. 118   B. 123   C. 128   D. 133

15.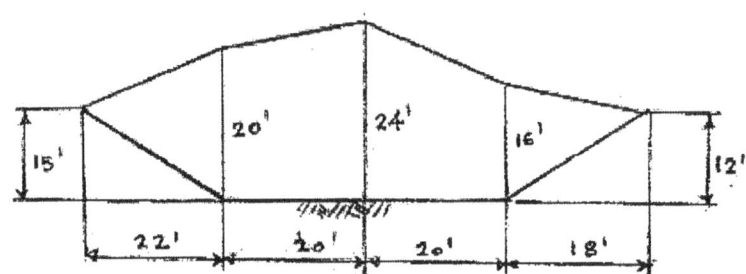

Shown above is the cut for a new highway at a given station. The area of the cut is _____ square feet.

A. 1204 B. 1224 C. 1244 D. 1264

16. The number of gallons of water in a cubic foot is

A. 7.33 B. 7.48 C. 8.00 D. 8.33

Questions 17-18.

DIRECTIONS: Questions 17 and 18 refer to a section across a city street.

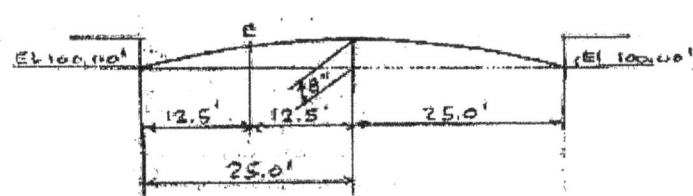

17. If the curve of the road is a parabola, the elevation of the road at point E is

A. 100.45 B. 100.50 C. 100.55 D. 100.60

18. The slope of "the road at E is _____ percent.

A. 2.00 B. 2.471 C. 2.667 D. 2.833

19. The universal lane width for a highway is _____ feet.

A. 10 to 11 B. 11 to 12 C. 12 to 13 D. 13 to 14

20. In unit price and lump sum contracts, contractors sometimes

A. reduce the unit price on items to be carried out early in the project and increase the unit price on items to be carried out later in the contract.
B. increase the unit price on items to be carried out early in the contract and reduce the unit price on items carried out later in the contract
C. reduce the unit price and increase the price on lump sum items
D. increase the price on unit items and decrease the price on lump sum items

Questions 21 to 23.

DIRECTIONS: Questions 21 to 23, inclusive, refer to the diagram below.

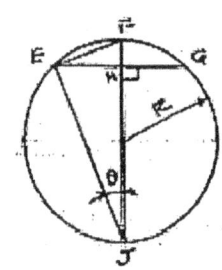

21. EF is equal to

    A. 2R sin θ B. 2R cos θ C. 2R tan θ D. 2R cot θ

22. EH is equal to

    A. R sin 2θ B. R cos 2θ C. R tan 2θ D. R cot 2θ

23. FH is equal to

    A. 2R sin θ cos θ/2
    C. 2R sin² θ
    B. 2R sin θ/2 cos θ
    D. 2R cos θ cos θ/2

24. The specifications state that the temperature shall be above 10° C. The temperature, in degrees Fahrenheit, is

    A. 40 B. 45 C. 50 D. 55

25. In a welding electrode designated by four numbers, the strength of the material in the electrode is shown in the _____ number(s).

    A. first
    C. first three
    B. first two
    D. four

KEY (CORRECT ANSWERS)

1. B
2. A
3. C
4. B
5. C

6. D
7. A
8. A
9. D
10. A

11. D
12. B
13. C
14. D
15. A

16. B
17. B
18. C
19. C
20. B

21. A
22. A
23. C
24. C
25. B

TEST 3

DIRECTIONS: Each question or incomplete statement is followed by several suggested answers or completions. Select the one that BEST answers the question or completes the statement. *PRINT THE LETTER OF THE CORRECT ANSWER IN THE SPACE AT THE RIGHT.*

1. Of the following elements, the one that is harmful in steel is   1.____
   - A. molybdenum
   - B. vandium
   - C. silicon
   - D. phosphorus

2. The size of a fillet weld shown at the right is designated by   2.____
   - A. A
   - B. B
   - C. C
   - D. D

3. The circle on the welding symbol means   3.____
   - A. weld in shop
   - B. weld in field
   - C. plug weld
   - D. weld all around

4. Stainless steel is designated as 18-8. The steel contains   4.____
   - A. 18% vanadium, 8% chromium
   - B. 18% chromium, 8% vanadium
   - C. 18% nickel, 8% chromium
   - D. 18% chromium, 8% nickel

5. Asphalt cements can be designated by one of two methods. One is viscosity, and the other is   5.____
   - A. liquidity
   - B. penetration
   - C. elasticity
   - D. ductility

6. Paving asphalts are measured by viscosity. A unit measure of absolute viscosity is   6.____
   - A. poise
   - B. tesla
   - C. oersted
   - D. pascal

7. The one of the following solvents that is NOT used in cutback asphalt is   7.____
   - A. naphtha
   - B. gasoline
   - C. toluene
   - D. kerosene

8. The advantage of using cutback asphalt over ordinary asphalt is that cutback asphalt _____ than ordinary asphalt.   8.____
   - A. has a higher viscosity
   - B. cures more slowly

C. can be applied at a temperature lower
D. produces a harder surfac

9. When excavating for a roadway, the volume of excavation removed becomes greater than the volume of the earth before removal. The percent of increase in volume is termed

A. swell
B. expansion
C. blow-up
D. displacement

9.____

10. The approximate increase in volume when dry sand is excavated is MOST NEARLY _____ percent.

A. 2
B. 20
C. 28
D. 36

10.____

11. The tolerance for the elevation of the base of a pavement is .02 feet. In the metric system, this would be

A. ± 4
B. ± 6
C. ± 8
D. ± 10

11.____

12. When the areas of a road surface to be patched are numerous, or they extend over a considerable area, it is often more efficient to recondition the entire surface.
The usual procedure is to _____ the surface of the roadway to the full depth of the surface material.

A. excavate
B. eviscerate
C. scarify
D. plow

12.____

13. The ASTM defines a permeable textile material or any other geotechnical engineering-related material as a

A. geomorphic material
B. synthetic permeable textile
C. geomorphic reinforcement
D. geotextile

13.____

14. In wood terminology, a shake is a

A. variation from a true or plane surface
B. separation along the grain
C. deviation edgewise from a straight line drawn from end to end of a piece
D. lack of wood or bark from any cause

14.____

15. The primary difference between heartwood and sapwood is that

A. heartwood is stronger than sapwood
B. sapwood is stronger than heartwood
C. sapwood is more susceptible to decay than heartwood
D. sapwood is normally darker than heartwood

15.____

16. The specific gravity of southern yellow pine based on oven-dry weight and volume is

A. .38
B. .48
C. G. .58
D. .68

16.____

17. The length of a 10 penny nail is _____ inches.

A. 3
B. 3 1/4
C. 3 1/2
D. 4

17.____

18. The specifications state that in extreme situations face brick may be cleaned with a 5% solution of muriatic acid. Muriatic acid is another name for _____ acid.

    A. sulfuric
    B. hydrochloric
    C. acetic
    D. hydrofluoric

19. The main advantage of CPM over the traditional bar chart in scheduling a construction project is that CPM can more easily

    A. procure material
    B. eliminate potential bottlenecks during construction
    C. improve safety on the project
    D. eliminate unnecessary work to complete the project

20. In CPM, the float is

    A. positive in the critical path
    B. negative in the critical path
    C. 0 in the critical path
    D. positive or negative in the critical path, depending on whether the project is ahead of schedule or behind schedule

21. In CPM, the float in a given activity is the

    A. uncertainty when the activity can be finished without delaying the project
    B. uncertainty as to how much time is needed to complete the activity
    C. period during which the activity can be started without delaying the project
    D. flexibility needed to complete the activity without delaying the project

22. The GREATEST source of construction-related claims for additional payment for contractors and cost overruns result from

    A. labor strikes
    B. errors in design
    C. unanticipated soil conditions
    D. faulty material

23. High early strength cement is used in a concrete mix whenever the extra cost is offset by the value of the earlier use of the structure. The use of additional Portland cement in a mix gives high early strength, but has the disadvantage of

    A. causing segregation when placing the concrete
    B. having reduced strength over a longer period of time
    C. requires more fine aggregates
    D. causing greater shrinkage of the mass in curing

24. Special cements are designed specifically to resist chemical attack. The chemical group it is designed to resist are

    A. chlorates
    B. sulfates
    C. nitrates
    D. carbonates

25. Of the following, the synthetic fiber LEAST likely to raise loads in slings is   25._____

   A. nylon
   B. orlon
   C. polyester
   D. polypropylene

KEY (CORRECT ANSWERS)

1. D	11. B
2. C	12. C
3. D	13. D
4. D	14. B
5. B	15. C
6. A	16. C
7. C	17. A
8. C	18. B
9. A	19. B
10. A	20. C

21. C
22. C
23. D
24. B
25. B

TEST 4

DIRECTIONS: Each question or incomplete statement is followed by several suggested answers or completions. Select the one that BEST answers the question or completes the statement. *PRINT THE LETTER OF THE CORRECT ANSWER IN THE SPACE AT THE RIGHT.*

1. Of the following liquids, the one that has the LOWEST viscosity is

   A. alcohol
   B. water
   C. raw petroleum
   D. glycerin

2. The inspector uses a sling psychrometer in check painting to check the

   A. density of the paint
   B. viscosity of the paint
   C. moisture in the air
   D. barometric pressure

3. Of the following tests on structural steel, the one that is NOT non-destructive is

   A. radiographic
   B. ultrasonic
   C. magnetic particle
   D. tensile

4. Which of the following is a high strength bolt?

   A. A7   B. A36   C. A325   D. A502

5. The size of hole for a 3/4 inch bolt is

   A. 3/4"
   B. 13/32"
   C. 13/16"
   D. 27/32"

6. Foam fire extinguishers are unsuitable to fight _____ fires.

   A. wood
   B. paper
   C. flammable liquid
   D. electric equipment

7. Of the following types of fire extinguishers, the one MOST suitable to fight wood and paper fires is

   A. water type-soda acid
   B. carbon dioxide
   C. sodium bicarbonate-dry chemical
   D. potassium bicarbonate-dry chemical

8. A multi-purpose fire extinguisher is

   A. foam
   B. carbon dioxide
   C. ABC
   D. soda acid

9. The fire extinguisher with the SHORTEST range is

A. cartridge operated B. soda acid
C. carbon dioxide D. stored pressure

10. The Occupational Safety and Health Act Part 1926 states that all trenches and earth embankments over _____ feet deep beoadequately protected against caving in.

    A. 4   B. 5   C. 6   D. 7

11. During excavation, most cave-ins occur

    A. when excavating for retaining walls
    B. during cold weather
    C. in shallow excavations
    D. in the western part of the United States

12. _____ soils are MOST susceptible to cave-ins.

    A. All   B. Clayey   C. Silty   D. Sandy

13. In highway construction work, material required for earthwork construction in excess of the quantity of suitable material available from the required grading, cuts and elevations is known as

    A. overhaul B. deficit
    C. borrow D. shrinkage

14. The number of strands in manila rope is USUALLY

    A. 2   B. 3   C. 4   D. 5

15. The factor of safety for manila rope is

    A. 3   B. 5   C. 7   D. 9

Questions 16-20.

DIRECTIONS: Questions 16 through 20, inclusive, refer to a section through a 20'-0" long reinforced concrete retaining wall.

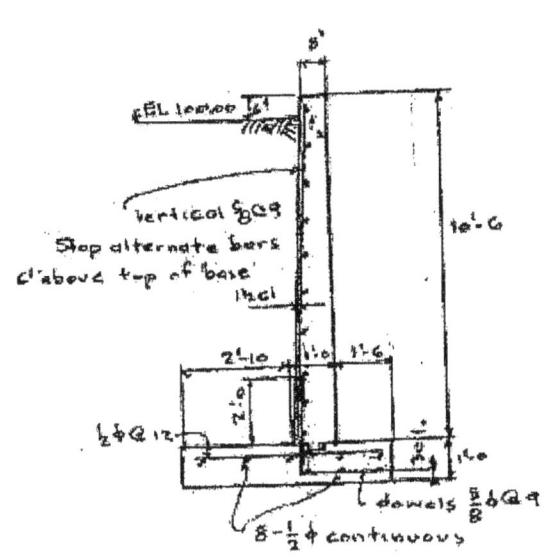

16. The slope of the inclined wall is MOST NEARLY 16.____
    A. 1/8 inch on 12"   B. 1/4 inch on 12"
    C. 3/8 inch on 12"   D. 1/2 inch on 12"

17. The volume of concrete in the vertical wall is _____ _____ cubic yards. 17.____
    A. 5.9   B. 6.1   C. 6.3   D. 6.5

18. The elevation of the bottom of the footing is 18.____
    A. 89.00'   B. 89.500'   C. 90.00'   D. 90.5'

19. The number of dowels ' a is 19.____
    A. 23   B. 25   C. 27   D. 29

20. The number of vertical '-a that are the full height of the wall is 20.____
    A. 12   B. 14   C. 16   D. 27

21. A state highway contract contains a Buy America clause. The material referred to in the clause is MOST NEARLY 21.____
    A. cement   B. lumber
    C. aluminum   D. steel

22. In a unit price contract where additional work does not fall under any item, the extra work is to be paid on a cost-plus basis. If the contractor uses his own crane, he is entitled to the 22.____
    A. cost of operating the crane only
    B. cost of operating the crane and servicing the crane only
    C. rental cost of the crane, the cost of operating the crane, and the cost of servicing the crane only
    D. cost of repairing the crane if the crane is damaged and the cost of operating and servicing the crane only

23. The delivery ticket for a truck delivering bituminous pavement mixture contains an entry "Tare Weight." Tare weight on the ticket refers to the 23.____
    A. correction for the scales weighing the bituminous mixture
    B. truck weight without load
    C. weight of fuel on the truck
    D. truck weight with load

24. The PRIMARY difference between silt and loam is that 24.____
    A. silt contains some organic material
    B. loam contains some organic material
    C. silt consists primarily of clay
    D. loam consists primarily of clay

25. A recent development in high strength concrete is _____ concrete. 25.____

    A. silica fume   B. low slump
    C. fly ash   D. finely ground cement

KEY (CORRECT ANSWERS)

1.	A	11.	C
2.	C	12.	A
3.	D	13.	C
4.	C	14.	B
5.	B	15.	B
6.	D	16.	C
7.	A	17.	D
8.	C	18.	A
9.	C	19.	C
10.	B	20.	B

21. D
22. C
23. B
24. B
25. A

EXAMINATION SECTION
TEST 1

DIRECTIONS: Each question or incomplete statement is followed by several suggested answers or completions. Select the one that BEST answers the question or completes the statement. *PRINT THE LETTER OF THE CORRECT ANSWER IN THE SPACE AT THE RIGHT.*

1. Reflective cracks in asphalt overlays 1.____

   A. are cracks in asphalt overlays that show the crack pattern of the pavement underneath
   B. are cracks that reflect caused by weakness in the base soil
   C. are the result of change in weights and frequency of truck travel in that they are greater than the loads the pavement was designed for
   D. reflect the type of cracks that normally could be expected for this type of pavement

2. In a guide for the estimation of Pavement Condition Rating for asphalt concrete pavement on a highway is the following classification: *Pavement is in fairly good condition with frequent slight cracking or very slight channeling and a few areas with slight alligatoring. Rideability is fairly good with intermittent rough and uneven sections.* The maintenance recommendation for this class of pavement condition is 2.____

   A. no maintenance required
   B. normal maintenance only
   C. resurface in 3 to 5 years
   D. resurface within 3 years

3. A major problem in bituminous asphalt plants is 3.____

   A. varying water content in the bituminous aggregate
   B. accuracy in the weighing equipment
   C. air pollution caused by plant exhausts
   D. producing a uniform mixture

4. The primary difference between asphalt concrete and sheet asphalt is asphalt concrete 4.____

   A. uses a finer sand than sheet asphalt
   B. uses a lower viscosity asphalt than sheet asphalt
   C. generally has a thinner layer than sheet asphalt
   D. contains coarse aggregate whereas sheet asphalt does not have coarse aggregate

5. It is common practice to apply a prime coat over untreated and some treated bases before asphalt concrete is placed. Of the following, the reasons for applying a prime coat are to 5.____

   A. bind loose particles of the base and minimize heat loss in the applied asphalt concrete
   B. act as a bond between base and pavement and prevent loss of asphalt in the asphalt concrete due to seepage
   C. deter rising moisture from penetrating the pavement and minimize heat loss in the applied asphalt concrete
   D. bind loose particles in the base and deter rising moisture from penetrating the asphalt pavement

6. The asphalt content of open graded mixes is generally at

   A. the same level as dense graded asphalt
   B. a higher level than dense graded asphalt
   C. a lower level than dense graded asphalt
   D. at a higher or lower level than dense graded asphalt depending on the percent of fine aggregate in the open graded asphalt mix

7. Sheet asphalt was extensively used in the past with a thickness of _____ inch(es).

   A. 1/2   B. 3/4   C. 1   D. 1 1/2

8. The progressive separation of aggregate particles in a pavement from the surface downward or from the edges inward in an asphalt concrete pavement is known as

   A. raveling   B. spalling
   C. scaling   D. reflective cracks

9. A profilometer used on an asphalt concrete road measures the _____ the road.

   A. grade of   B. roughness of
   C. impact resistance of D. channels in

10. Reinforcing steel is used in a footing. The minimum distance the bottom of the steel is above the subgrade should be _____ inch(es).

    A. 1   B. 2   C. 3   D. 4

11. Loose sand weighs 120 pounds per cubic foot and the specific gravity of sand is 2.65. The absolute volume of a cubic foot of loose sand is, in cubic feet, most nearly

    A. .73   B. .75   C. .77   D. .79

12. The maximum size of coarse aggregate in a concrete mix for a reinforced concrete structure is determined by the size of the concrete section and the

    A. type of cement used
    B. proportion of fine aggregate
    C. minimum distance between reinforcing bars
    D. yield point of the reinforcing steel

13. Cement (High Early Strength) is Type _____ cement.

    A. I   B. II   C. III   D. IV

14. Slunp in concrete is a measure of

    A. strength   B. porosity
    C. permeability   D. workability

15. The cross section area of a #8 bar is _____ square inches.

    A. .60   B. .79   C. 1.00   D. 1.25

16. Construction joints for slabs in a building shall be made

    A. at the supports
    B. within 1/8 of the span of the slab from the supports
    C. from 1/8 to 3/8 of the span of the slab from the supports
    D. near the center of the span

17. Chutes for depositing concrete shall have a slope no greater than

    A. 1   B. 1½   C. 2   D. 2½

18. Air entrained cement is used in a concrete mix on highways primarily to

    A. make the concrete stronger after 28 days
    B. have a higher early strength
    C. make the surface more resistant to freezing and thawing
    D. make the surface less porous to better resist the impact of trucks

19. Beach sand is unsuitable as a fine aggregate in concrete because it has salt contamination and the sand particles are

    A. smooth   B. rough
    C. uniform in size   D. too fine

20. The fineness modulus of sand for concrete is taken on the job to insure

    A. the quality of the sand
    B. that the gradation of the sand does not change
    C. that there is not an excess of fines in the sand
    D. that there is not an excess of oversized particles in the sand

21. The coarse and fine aggregate for concrete are usually tested

    A. at the quarry site
    B. at the job site
    C. by sampling a loaded truck
    D. in the design engineering office

22. The slump in concrete for highway mixtures range from _____ inches.

    A. 1 to 3   B. 2 to 5   C. 3 to 6   D. 4 to 7

23. A bag of cement weighs _____ pounds.

    A. 90   B. 94   C. 97   D. 100

24. The design strength of concrete is to be reached at the end of _____ days.

    A. 7   B. 14   C. 21   D. 28

25. Of the following, water-cement ratio may be defined as _____ of water per _____ of cement.

    A. gallons; bag   B. gallons; 100 pounds
    C. quarts; bag   D. quarts; 100 pounds

KEY (CORRECT ANSWERS)

1. A
2. C
3. C
4. D
5. D

6. B
7. D
8. A
9. B
10. C

11. A
12. C
13. C
14. D
15. B

16. D
17. C
18. C
19. C
20. B

21. A
22. A
23. B
24. D
25. A

TEST 2

DIRECTIONS: Each question or incomplete statement is followed by several suggested answers or completions. Select the one that BEST answers the question or completes the statement. *PRINT THE LETTER OF THE CORRECT ANSWER IN THE SPACE AT THE RIGHT.*

1. The maximum size of coarse aggregate in a concrete mix for a reinforced concrete structure is determined by the size of the section and the

   A. type of cement used
   B. proportion of fine aggregate
   C. minimum distance between reinforcing bars
   D. the yield point of the reinforcing steel

1.____

Questions 2-3.

DIRECTIONS: Questions 2 and 3 refer to concrete mix design.

2. The present and most popular method of rational mixture design is sponsored by ACI committee 211, 1994. In this method, the design using ordinary cement is based on

   A. slump and water-cement ratio
   B. aggregate size and water-cement ratio
   C. slump, aggregate size, and water-cement ratio
   D. slump and water content

2.____

3. In the method of mix design of ACI committee 211, 1994, water content is expressed in

   A. pounds of water per bag of cement
   B. pounds of water per cubic foot of concrete
   C. gallons of water per cubic yard of concrete
   D. pounds of water per cubic yard of concrete

3.____

4. The right to use or control the property of another for designated purposes is the definition of

   A. property acquisition   B. right-of-way
   C. an air right   D. an easement

4.____

5. A 24 inch circular drainage pipe is shown on a profile drawing of a highway as an ellipse with the major axis vertical. The reason for this is

   A. the horizontal and vertical scales of the profile drawing are different
   B. the pipe is not perpendicular to the center line of the roadway
   C. to emphasize the height of the pipe
   D. the slope of the pipe is taken into account

5.____

6. On a highway plan is a note for #4 wire game fence reading Lt Sta 2970 + 00 to 2979 + 85, Rt Sta 2970 + 00 to 2980 + 70. The total number of linear feet of new #4 wire game fence is, in feet, most nearly

   A. 1955   B. 2005   C. 2055   D. 2105

6.____

7. The superelevation of a curve is .075 feet. The superelevation, in inches, is most nearly

   A. 9   B. 5/8   C. 3/4   D. 7/8

8. On a plan for a highway is a note $\dfrac{\text{S.C.}}{\text{Sta } 2968+56.50}$ The S.C. is an abbreviation for

   A. slope at curve
   B. spiral to circular curve
   C. superelevated curve
   D. separation at center

9. Of the following methods of soil stabilization for the base of a highway pavement, the one that is most effective is

   A. a cement admixture
   B. a lime admixture
   C. an emulsified asphalt treated soil
   D. mechanical soil stabilization

10. An asphalt pavement mixture having a brownish dull appearance and lacking a shiny black luster

    A. is normal for an asphalt mixture
    B. contains too little aggregate
    C. is too cold
    D. contains too little asphalt

11. Steam rising from an asphalt mix when it is dumped into a hopper indicates

    A. there is excessive moisture in the aggregate
    B. the mix is overheated
    C. emulsification is taking place
    D. the mixture has not been adequately mixed

12. The disadvantage of excessive fine aggregate in an asphalt mix is

    A. it is difficult to get a uniform mix
    B. it will require an excessive amount of asphalt
    C. it is difficult to apply because of the grittiness of the mix
    D. the final surface will tend to be rough

13. On highways where heavy trucks are permitted, the percent of total traffic that are heavy trucks is, in percent, MOST NEARLY

    A. 4   B. 11   C. 18   D. 25

14. A single axle 80 kN load is equal to _____ pounds per axle.

    A. 12,000   B. 14,000   C. 16,000   D. 18,000

15. Normal traffic growth in the United States is _____ percent per year.

    A. 1-2   B. 3-5   C. 5-7   D. 7-9

16. EAL is an abbreviation for _____ axle load

    A. equal
    B. equivalent
    C. effective
    D. estimated

17. A roughometer is a single-wheeled trailer instrumented to measure the roughness of a pavement surface. The measure is in inches per   17.____

    A. foot   B. yard   C. hundred yards   D. mile

18. The Atterberg Limit is a test on   18.____

    A. coarse aggregate   B. asphalt
    C. soil   D. Portland cement

19. Of the following, the one that is a high strength bolt is designated   19.____

    A. A7   B. A36   C. A180   D. A325

20. Construction contracts in a broad sense fall into two categories - fixed price and   20.____

    A. cost-plus   B. fixed price plus overhead and profit
    C. negotiated price   D. arbitrated price

21. A punch list on a construction job is usually made by the inspector   21.____

    A. weekly
    B. monthly
    C. continuously during the last half of the job
    D. near the end of the job

22. When an accident occurs on a construction job in which someone is injured, an accident report is usually made out by the   22.____

    A. insurance carrier   B. contractor
    C. inspector   D. inspector's superior

23. The inspector and the contractor share common goals. The one of the goals listed below that is NOT shared by the contractor and the inspector is   23.____

    A. get a good job done
    B. see that the contractor makes a reasonable profit
    C. get the job done as speedily as possible
    D. have the job done at as low a cost as possible

24. A crack relief layer is placed over an existing Portland cement concrete pavement followed by a well-graded intermediate course, then a dense graded surface course. The crack relief layer consists of an open graded   24.____

    A. mix of 100% crushed material with 25-35% interconnected voids
    B. crushed material heavily compacted with no binder
    C. hot mix made up of 80% crushed material with 20% shredded rubber
    D. dense crushed material with voids filled by asphalt

25. Most of the major work performed on the nation's bridges involves   25.____

    A. painting the bridges
    B. upgrading the bridges to carry heavier loads
    C. replacing the concrete decks
    D. replacing the suspenders on cable supported bridges

KEY (CORRECT ANSWERS)

1. C
2. C
3. D
4. D
5. A

6. C
7. D
8. B
9. A
10. D

11. A
12. B
13. B
14. D
15. B

16. B
17. D
18. C
19. D
20. A

21. D
22. B
23. B
24. A
25. C

EXAMINATION SECTION
TEST 1

DIRECTIONS: Each question or incomplete statement is followed by several suggested answers or completions. Select the one that BEST answers the question or completes the statement. *PRINT THE LETTER OF THE CORRECT ANSWER IN THE SPACE AT THE RIGHT.*

1. It is the policy of the department to hold each inspector responsible for formal work assignments given to him.
   Of the following, the BEST reason for this is that it
   A. enables division personnel to keep track of the work schedule
   B. encourages inspectors to be careful with written documents
   C. increases the speed with which inspections are carried out
   D. provides a double check on the time sheet records of inspectors

   1.____

2. Assume that you are faced with delays caused by absences of team members due to illness.
   Of the following, the BEST means of handling this problem is to
   A. have your team members keep an accurate record of their absences so that you will be able to identify anyone who is becoming accident-prone
   B. insist on prompt notification at all times when someone on your tea is absent because of illness
   C. require that your team members submit a memorandum informing you of the days on which they will be absent
   D. take over all tasks assigned to your team members when they are absent

   2.____

3. Assume that one of the men on your team tells you that he has a problem and would like to discuss it with you privately. During the course of this meeting, it becomes apparent that the man's difficulty stems from conflicts he is having with his wife.
   Of the following, the BEST course of action that you, his supervisor, should take in this situation is to
   A. advise the employee to meet with your superior, who might be able to give him more objective advice
   B. gather enough facts to advise the man about definite solutions for his problem
   C. help the man analyze what the problem is but leave the decision to him
   D. tell the man that you can talk to him only about problems that are job-related

   3.____

4. Sometimes it may be advantageous for a senior inspector to let the inspectors under his supervision participate in the development of decisions that must be made about the team's activities.
   The one of the following that is LEAST likely to result when team members participate in supervisory decisions is that the inspectors may

   4.____

A. be able to show leadership
B. have a chance to feel creative
C. require closer supervision
D. take more responsibility for minor problems

5. Of the following, the CHIEF reason that the senior inspector should take disciplinary measures as soon as possible after a subordinate inspector's violation of department rules is that
    A. delay will make the senior inspector seem lax
    B. the inspector is more likely to accept the discipline a justified
    C. the supervisor may forget about the offense
    D. there is less likelihood that other inspectors will find out about the offense

5.____

6. Assume that you have been directed to institute a new procedure for writing reports about violations encountered during the inspections conducted by the team of which you are in charge. You have heard, through the grapevine, that several of the experienced inspectors on the team have objections to this new procedure.
Of the following, the BEST course of action for you to take FIRST in this situation is to
    A. issue a written order to put the new procedure into effect
    B. meet with all the inspectors on your team to discuss the procedure
    C. modify the procedure to make it acceptable to all of your inspectors
    D. postpone institution of the new procedure

6.____

7. Assume that the head of your unit expects to be out for a week because of illness. You are to act as head of the unit for that time.
In determining what to do about those inspection duties that you were originally scheduled to perform and which should not be postponed, it would be MOST advisable to
    A. assign them to the inspector who needs training in this area
    B. assign them to the inspector with the most seniority
    C. attempt to do as many of them as possible yourself
    D. divide them among all inspectors who have the time and ability

7.____

8. The one of the following situations that is LEAST likely to result from poor planning and organization of an inspection unit's work is that
    A. inspectors will be uncertain about their responsibilities
    B. job performance will be poor
    C. the work will be completed at a steady monotonous pace
    D. there will be a high turnover rate in the unit's staff

8.____

9. Of the following, the BEST course of action to take in order to avoid charges of favoritism when making job assignments is to
    A. delegate the authority to make assignments to a well-liked experienced inspector
    B. keep records which may demonstrate proper distribution and rotation of assignments

9.____

C. select the oldest inspectors for the most desirable assignments
D. tell the men that, if they have any gripes about their assignments, they should see the supervising inspector

10. Of the following, the MOST important reason for a senior inspector to receive communications from the supervising inspector before they are transmitted to the inspectors is that he can
    A. avoid discussing communications with his subordinates
    B. exercises close supervision over every detail of the inspectors' assignments
    C. limit the amount of information received by his subordinates
    D. maintains his position in the chain of command

10._____

11. If an organization has rules that are clear but excessively detailed and rigid, the one of the following which is MOST likely to occur is that
    A. employees will tend to ignore the rules
    B. records of performance will be more difficult to maintain
    C. supervisors will have more difficulty in applying the rules to individual situations
    D. use of individual judgment and discretion will be decreased

11._____

12. An effective senior inspector strives to build up the feeling that he and his men are on the same team. The imposition of discipline may serious endanger the relationship built up between him and his men.
    The one of the following steps that the senior inspector may take to insure that the imposition of discipline will NOT cause any deterioration of his relationship with his subordinates is to
    A. avoid disciplinary action, except for very serious offenses
    B. delegate simple disciplinary problems to a competent, experienced inspector
    C. discipline his men in groups so that they will feel as if they were part of a team
    D. impose discipline in as impersonal way as possible

12._____

13. Suppose that one of the inspectors under the supervision of a senior inspector is repeatedly late for work. Despite the inspector's habitual lateness, he manages to complete his work assignments on schedule.
    Of the following, the MOST advisable action for the senior inspector to take in this situation is to
    A. ask one of the other inspectors to speak to him about his attendance
    B. ignore the inspector's habitual lateness as long as he does his work properly
    C. reprimand the inspector privately and follow through to see whether his attendance improves
    D. tell him in the presence of the other inspectors that he must improve his attendance record

13._____

14. Assume that you are informed by your superior that all reports prepared by your team should be checked by you when possible before their submission to a supervising inspector.
    Of the following, the BEST course of action to take if you are too busy to look at all these reports and they have to be sent out right away is to
    A. delegate the responsibility for checking the reports to someone you have carefully instructed in the need for neat and accurate reports
    B. request additional staff from another unit to help you review these reports
    C. send the reports out without checking them and attach an explanatory note, telling your superior that you have not had time to look at them
    D. tell our men to review one another's reports and initial them

15. Assume that a senior inspector notices that another senior inspector divides his team's workload in what seems to him to be an inefficient manner. He decides to report this to the supervising inspector.
    Of the following, an accurate evaluation of the action taken by the senior inspector in this situation is that it is GENERALLY
    A. *good* practice, mainly because the supervising inspector is the only person authorized to make this senior inspector divide the work according to standard procedure
    B. *good* practice, mainly because the senior inspector needs close supervision to adequately carry out his responsibilities
    C. *poor* practice, mainly because the senior inspector should have consulted other senior inspectors about this situation
    D. *poor* practice, mainly because the senior inspector should understand that other senior inspectors may manage their operations differently

16. Assume that you have heard a rumor that department rules are about to be changed in a manner which will make certain types of inspections more complicated.
    Of the following, the BEST action for you to take in this situation is to
    A. ask the members of your staff, individually, if they have heard such a rumor
    B. call a meeting of your staff to tell them such a change is rumored
    C. make plans to change your unit's procedures to adapt to the new methods
    D. await official confirmation or denial of the rumor

17. Assume that one of the inspectors under your supervision has been doing an excellent job but no longer seems to have any interest in the work. He complains to you that he finds the work boring.
    Of the following, the MOST advisable action for you to take FIRST is to
    A. ask some of his fellow inspectors to discuss the matter with him
    B. attempt to vary his assignments and give him more complex assignments
    C. remind him that his evaluation by superiors may depend in part on the interest he shows in his work
    D. suggest that the inspector be transferred to another division

18. The BEST way for you to prepare the inspectors in your unit to handle special assignments speedily and make decisions in an emergency is to
    A. follow each employee's work very carefully so you know where he is least efficient
    B. give them the freedom to make decisions in their everyday work
    C. refuse to accept work that is turned in late
    D. set deadlines ahead of the time when regularly assigned work is actually due so they will learn to work efficiently

18.____

19. Suppose you are supervising several inspectors. One of the inspectors has recently transferred to your unit. You discover that although he generally prepares his reports in a fairly correct way, he does not follow the prescribed procedure that you have taught the other inspectors.
    In this situation, the one of the following that it would be BEST for you to do is to
    A. allow him to use his own procedure if it is accurate and efficient
    B. refer him to your supervisor
    C. discuss the matter with all the inspectors and let them decide which procedure they wish to follow
    D. tell him to follow the procedure used by the other inspectors

19.____

20. Assume that you have one of your most competent inspectors working on a new type of project. As you are reviewing his work, you notice he has made some errors.
    You should
    A. correct the errors yourself, otherwise the inspector will get discouraged
    B. ignore the errors; they are probably not important, especially when the inspector is first learning the job
    C. tell the inspector about the errors; he will probably learn from them
    D. tell the inspector about the errors; then he will be aware that he is careless

20.____

21. Assume that your unit has been given a special assignment to make an original study. You plan to give this assignment to two of your most competent inspectors.
    The BEST way to start them on this work is to
    A. ask the two inspectors how they think the work can be done in a most effective way
    B. do some of the work with the inspectors to make sure they do not make any mistakes
    C. tell the inspectors they will be held directly responsible for the success of the study
    D. write up detailed instructions and give them to the inspectors who will do the work

21.____

22. Of the following steps in setting up an employee training program, the one which should PRECEDE the others is to
    A. assemble all the materials needed in the training program
    B. decide what training methods would be most effective
    C. determine what facilities are available for training purposes
    D. outline the areas that would be covered in the training program

23. Assume that you find it necessary to retrain an older, experienced inspector because you are giving this inspector a different kind of assignment.
    Of the following, the problem that is MOST likely to arise when retraining such a staff member is that the
    A. instructor will have disciplinary problems with this employee
    B. instructor will know less than this staff member
    C. employee at this status often lacks motivation to be retrained
    D. younger men will be unable to keep up with the performance of this employee

24. Assume that an inspector has recently been transferred from another unit and is now on your team.
    Of the following, the BEST method for you to use to determine whether this man needs any additional instruction or training is to
    A. ask him whether he is having difficulty with the work you assign to him
    B. ask the man's former supervisor whether he was a competent inspector
    C. review the way he handles the various tasks that you assign to him
    D. send this man into the field with one of your inspectors and have him evaluate the newly assigned inspector

25. Instituting a program of on-the-job training may sometimes present problems for the supervisor because, when first initiated, such training
    A. does not take place under actual working conditions
    B. is less instructive than formal training sessions
    C. may result in a decrease in the authority of the supervisor
    D. may slow down the unit's work

26. Suppose that you are approached by a newly appointed inspector who asks you to make an inspection visit with him because he is unsure of the procedure.
    The one of the following that you should do FIRST is to
    A. agree to make the visit with him
    B. refer him to the supervisor for help
    C. report him to the supervisor for incorrect behavior
    D. tell him to do the best he can and offer to help him write up the report

27. Suppose that you are writing up your inspection reports in your office on a particular day. A fellow inspector, who has left his identification at home, asks if he may use your identification card and badge in order to perform his scheduled inspections.

Of the following, you should
- A. allow him to use your identification since he is an inspector
- B. offer to perform the inspections for him if he will write the reports
- C. refuse his request and suggest he explain the situation to the supervisor
- D. tell him you need your identification for yourself

28. Assume that you are assigned to handle telephone complaints. After you have attempted to handle a complaint from a belligerent caller, the caller asks your name, saying that he is going to report you to your superior for being insolent to him.
It would be BEST for you to
- A. give the caller a false name so he will stop bothering you
- B. give the caller your name and explain the circumstances to your superior afterwards
- C. refuse to give the caller your name
- D. tell the caller that you have not been insolent to him

29. As a senior inspector, you are permitted to hold an outside job as long as it is NOT
- A. dangerous
- B. in conflict with the performance of your inspection duties
- C. mentally or physically taxing
- D. paid at a rate higher than your inspector job

30. Of the following, the MOST important reason that graphs and charts are used in reports to present material that can be treated statistically is that such material
- A. is easier to understand when it is presented in graph or chart form
- B. looks more impressive when it is presented in graph or chart form
- C. requires less time to prepare when it is presented in a graph or chart form instead of written out
- D. take up less space in graph or chart form than when it is written out

KEY (CORRECT ANSWERS)

1.	A	11.	D	21.	A
2.	B	12.	D	22.	D
3.	C	13.	C	23.	C
4.	C	14.	A	24.	C
5.	B	15.	D	25.	D
6.	B	16.	D	26.	B
7.	D	17.	B	27.	C
8.	C	18.	B	28.	B
9.	B	19.	D	29.	B
10.	D	20.	C	30.	A

TEST 2

DIRECTIONS: Each question or incomplete statement is followed by several suggested answers or completions. Select the one that BEST answers the question or completes the statement. *PRINT THE LETTER OF THE CORRECT ANSWER IN THE SPACE AT THE RIGHT.*

1. If an inspector finds a discrepancy between the plans and specifications, he should
    A. always follow the plans
    B. ask for an interpretation
    C. always follow the specifications
    D. follow the plans if the difference is in dimensions

    1.____

2. In performing field inspectional work, an inspector is the contact man between the public and the agency, and it is his job to secure compliance through the maximum utilization of persuasion and education and the minimum application of coercion.
    According to this statement, an inspector performing inspectional duties should
    A. seek to obtain voluntary compliance and use coercion only as a last resort
    B. be conciliatory on all issues of non-compliance and not take an attitude of firmness and authority
    C. maintain a strictly impersonal attitude in the exercise of his duties at all times
    D. use the threat of legal action to secure conformance with specified requirements

    2.____

3. The BEST way for a supervising inspector to determine whether a new inspector is learning his work properly is to
    A. ask the other men how this man is making out
    B. question him directly on details of the work
    C. assume that if he asks no questions, he knows the work
    D. inspect and follow up on the work which is assigned to him

    3.____

4. In assigning his men to various jobs, the BEST principle for a supervising inspector to follow is to
    A. study the men's abilities and assign them accordingly
    B. rotate a man from job to job until you find one which he can do well
    C. assign each of them to a job and let them adjust to it in their own way
    D. assume that men appointed to the position can do all parts of the work equally well

    4.____

5. Good inspection methods require that the inspector
    A. be observant and check all details
    B. constantly check with the engineer who designed the job
    C. apply specifications according to his interpretations
    D. permit slight job variation to establish good public relations

    5.____

6. An inspector inspecting a large job under construction inspected plumbing at 9 A.M., heating at 10 A.M., and ventilation at 11 A.M., and did his officework in the afternoon. He followed the same pattern daily for months.
   This procedure is
   A. *bad*, because not enough time is devoted to plumbing
   B. *bad*, because the tradesmen know when the inspections will occur
   C. *good*, because it is methodical and he does not miss any of the trades
   D. *good*, because it gives equal amount of time to the important trades

6.____

7. The BEST way to evaluate the overall state of completion of a construction project is to check the progress estimate against the
   A. inspection worksheet   B. construction schedule
   C. inspector's checklist   D. equipment maintenance schedule

7.____

8. When a contractor fails to adhere to an approved progress schedule, he should
   A. revise the schedule without delay
   B. ask for an extension of time on account of delays
   C. adopt such additional means and methods of construction as will make up for time lost
   D. take no immediate action with the hope that sufficient time will be available later on that will assure the completion in accordance with the schedule

8.____

9. The usual contract for agency work includes a section entitled instructions to bidders, which states that the
   A. contractor agrees that he has made his own examination and will make no claim for damages on account of errors or omissions
   B. contractor shall not make claims for damages of any discrepancy, error or omission in any plans
   C. estimates of quantities and calculations are guaranteed by the agency to be correct and are deemed to be a representation of the conditions affecting the work
   D. plans, measurement, dimensions, and conditions under which the work is to be performed are guaranteed by the agency

9.____

10. A lump sum type of contract may require the contractor to submit a schedule of unit price.
    The BEST reason for this is that it
    A. prevents the lump sum from being too high
    B. simplifies the selection of the lowest bidder
    C. enables the estimators to check the total cost
    D. provides a means of making equitable partial payments

10.____

11. A contractor on a large construction project USUALLY receives partial payments based on
    A. estimates of completed work
    B. actual cost of materials delivered and work completed
    C. estimates of material delivered and not paid for by the contractor
    D. the breakdown estimate submitted after the contract was signed and prorated over the estimated duration of the contract

11.____

12. In order to avoid disputes over payments for extra work in a contract for construction, the BEST procedure to follow would be to
    A. have contractor submit work progress reports daily
    B. insert a special clause in the contract specifications
    C. have a representative on the job at all times to verify conditions
    D. allocate a certain percentage of the cost of the job to cover such expenses

12.____

13. A fixed amount of money is generally withheld from the contractor for a definite period after the completion of construction.
    The BEST reason for this is
    A. that the money will be available for taxes due
    B. to penalize the contractor for poor work
    C. that it is a security for the repair of any defective work
    D. that the money will be available for modifications in the design of the structure

13.____

14. Prior to the installation of equipment called for in the specifications, the contractor is USUALLY required to submit for approval
    A. sets of shop drawings
    B. a set of revised specifications
    C. a detailed description of the methods of work to be used
    D. a complete list of skilled and unskilled tradesmen he proposes to use

14.____

15. During the actual construction work, the CHIEF value of a construction schedule is to
    A. insure that the work will be done on time
    B. reveal whether production is falling behind
    C. show how much equipment and material is required for the project
    D. furnish data as to the methods and techniques of construction operations

15.____

16. Of the following items, the one which should NOT be included in a proposed work schedule is
    A. a schedule of hourly wage rates and supplementary benefits
    B. an estimated time required for delivery of materials and equipment
    C. the anticipated commencement and completion of the various operations
    D. the sequence and inter-relationship of various operations with those of related contracts

16.____

4 (#2)

17. The frequency with which job reports are submitted should depend MAINLY on   17.____
    A. how comprehensive the report has to be
    B. the amount of information in the report
    C. the availability of an experienced man to write the report
    D. the importance of changes in the information included in the report

18. The CHIEF purpose in preparing an outline for a report is usually to insure that   18.____
    A. the report will be grammatically correct
    B. every point will be given equal emphasis
    C. principal and secondary points will be properly integrated
    D. the language of the report will be of the same level and include the same technical terms

19. The MAIN reason for requiring written job reports is to   19.____
    A. avoid the necessity of oral orders
    B. develop better methods of doing the work
    C. provide a permanent record of what was done
    D. increase the amount of work that can be done

20. Assume you are recommending in a report to your superior that a radical change in a standard maintenance procedure should be adopted.   20.____
    Of the following, the MOST important information to be included in this report is
    A. a list of the reasons for making this change
    B. the names of others who favor the change
    C. a complete description of the present procedure
    D. amount of training time needed for the new procedure

KEY (CORRECT ANSWERS)

1.	B		11.	A
2.	A		12.	C
3.	B		13.	C
4.	A		14.	A
5.	A		15.	B
6.	B		16.	A
7.	B		17.	D
8.	C		18.	C
9.	A		19.	C
10.	D		20.	A

WORK SCHEDULING

EXAMINATION SECTION
TEST 1

DIRECTIONS: Each question or incomplete statement is followed by several suggested answers or completions. Select the one that BEST answers the question or completes the statement. *PRINT THE LETTER OF THE CORRECT ANSWER IN THE SPACE AT THE RIGHT.*

Questions 1-6.

DIRECTIONS: Questions 1 through 6 are to be answered SOLELY on the basis of the information given in the ELEVATOR OPERATORS' WORK SCHEDULE shown below.

ELEVATOR OPERATORS' WORK SCHEDULE				
Operator	Hours of Work	A.M. Relief Period	Lunch Hour	P.M. Relief Period
Anderson	8:30-4:30	10:20-10:30	12:00-1:00	2:20-2:30
Carter	8:00-4:00	10:10-10:20	11:45-12:45	2:30-2:40
Daniels	9:00-5:00	10:20-10:30	12:30-1:30	3:15-3:25
Grand	9:30-5:30	11:30-11:40	1:00-2:00	4:05-4:15
Jones	7:45-3:45	9:45-9:55	11:30-12:30	2:05-2:15
Lewis	9:45-5:45	11:40-11:50	1:15-2:15	4:20-4:30
Nance	8:45-4:45	10:50-11:00	12:30-1:30	3:05-3:15
Perkins	8:00-4:00	10:00-10:10	12:00-1:00	2:40-2:50
Russo	7:45-3:45	9:30-9:40	11:30-12:30	2:10-2:20
Smith	9:45-5:45	11:45-11:55	1:15-2:15	4:05-4:15

1. The two operators who are on P.M. relief at the SAME time are

   A. Anderson and Daniels B. Carter and Perkins
   C. Jones and Russo   D. Grand and Smith

   1.____

2. Of the following, the two operators who have the SAME lunch hour are

   A. Anderson and Perkins B. Daniels and Russo
   C. Grand and Smith   D. Nance and Russo

   2.____

3. At 12:15, the number of operators on their lunch hour is

   A. 3   B. 4   C. 5   D. 6

   3.____

4. The operator who has an A.M. relief period right after Perkins and a P.M. relief period right before Perkins is

   A. Russo   B. Nance   C. Daniels   D. Carter

   4.____

5. The number of operators who are scheduled to be working at 4:40 is

   A. 5   B. 6   C. 7   D. 8

   5.____

103

6. According to the schedule, it is MOST correct to say that 6._____
   A. no operator has a relief period during the time that another operator has a lunch hour
   B. each operator has to wait an identical amount of time between the end of lunch and the beginning of P.M. relief period
   C. no operator has a relief period before 9:45 or after 4:00
   D. each operator is allowed a total of 1 hour and 20 minutes for lunch hour and relief periods

KEY (CORRECT ANSWERS)

1. D
2. A
3. C
4. D
5. A
6. D

TEST 2

DIRECTIONS: Each question or incomplete statement is followed by several suggested answers or completions. Select the one that BEST answers the question or completes the statement. *PRINT THE LETTER OF THE CORRECT ANSWER IN THE SPACE AT THE RIGHT.*

Questions 1-7.

DIRECTIONS: Questions 1 through 7 are to be answered SOLELY on the basis of the time sheet and instructions given below.

The following time sheet indicates the times that seven laundry workers arrived and left each day for the week of August 23. The times they arrived for work are shown under the heading IN, and the times they left are shown under the heading OUT. The letter (P) indicates time which was used for personal business. Time used for this purpose is charged to annual leave. Lunch time is one-half hour from noon to 12:30 P.M. and is not accounted for on this time record.

The employees on this shift are scheduled to work from 8:00 A.M. to 4:00 P.M. Lateness is charged to annual leave. Reporting after 8:00 A.M. is considered late.

	MON.		TUES.		WED.		THURS.		FRI.	
	AM IN	PM OUT	AM IN	PM OUT	AM IN	PM OUT	AM IN	PM OUT	AM IN	PM OUT
Baxter	7:50	4:01	7:49	4:07	8:00	4:07	8:20	4:00	7:42	4:03
Gardner	8:02	4:00	8:20	4:00	8:05	3:30(P)	8:00	4:03	8:00	4:07
Clements	8:00	4:04	8:03	4:01	7:59	4:00	7:54	4:06	7:59	4:00
Tompkins	7:56	4:00	Annual leave		8:00	4:07	7:59	4:00	8:00	4:01
Wagner	8:04	4:03	7:40	4:00	7:53	4:04	8:00	4:09	7:53	4:00
Patterson	8:00	2:30(P)	8:15	4:04	Sick leave		7:45	4:00	7:59	4:04
Cunningham	7:43	4:02	7:50	4:00	7:59	4:02	8:00	4:10	8:00	4:00

1. Which one of the following laundry workers did NOT have any time charged to annual leave or sick leave during the week?   1._____

     A. Gardner   B. Clements   C. Tompkins   D. Cunningham

2. On which day did ALL the laundry workers arrive on time?   2._____

     A. Monday   B. Wednesday   C. Thursday   D. Friday

3. Which of the following laundry workers used time to take care of personal business?   3._____

     A. Baxter and Clements   B. Patterson and Cunningham
     C. Gardner and Patterson   D. Wagner and Tompkins

4. How many laundry workers were late on Monday?   4._____

     A. 1   B. 2   C. 3   D. 4

5. Which one of the following laundry workers arrived late on three of the five days?   5._____

     A. Baxter   B. Gardner   C. Wagner   D. Patterson

6. The percentage of laundry workers reporting to work late on Tuesday is MOST NEARLY   6.____
   A. 15%   B. 25%   C. 45%   D. 50%

7. The percentage of laundry workers that were absent for an entire day during the week is MOST NEARLY   7.____
   A. 6%   B. 9%   C. 15%   D. 30%

KEY (CORRECT ANSWERS)

1. D
2. D
3. C
4. B
5. B
6. C
7. D

TEST 3

Questions 1-9.

DIRECTIONS: Questions 1 through 9 are to be answered SOLELY on the basis of the following information and timesheet given below.

The following is a foreman's timesheet for his crew for one week. The hours worked each day or the reason the man was off on that day are shown on the sheet. *R* means rest day. *A* means annual leave. *S* means sick leave. Where a man worked only part of a day, both the number of hours worked and the number of hours taken off are entered. The reason for absence is entered in parentheses next to the number of hours taken off.

Name	Saturday	Sunday	Monday	Tuesday	Wednesday	Thursday	Friday
Smith	R	R	7	7	7	3 4(A)	7
Jones	R	7	7	7	7	7	R
Green	R	R	7	7	S	S	S
White	R	R	7	7	A	7	7
Doe	7	7	7	7	7	R	R
Brown	R	R	A	7	7	7	7
Black	R	R	S	7	7	7	7
Reed	R	R	7	7	7	7	S
Roe	R	R	A	7	7	7	7
Lane	7	R	R	7	7	A	S

1. The caretaker who worked EXACTLY 21 hours during the week is   1._____

   A. Lane   B. Roe   C. Smith   D. White

2. The TOTAL number of hours worked by all caretakers during the week is   2._____

   A. 268   B. 276   C. 280   D. 288

3. The two days of the week on which MOST caretakers were off are   3._____

   A. Thursday and Friday   B. Friday and Saturday
   C. Saturday and Sunday   D. Sunday and Monday

4. The day on which three caretakers were off on sick leave is   4._____

   A. Monday   B. Friday   C. Saturday   D. Sunday

5. The two workers who took LEAST time off during the week are   5._____

   A. Doe and Reed   B. Jones and Doe
   C. Reed and Smith   D. Smith and Jones

6. The caretaker who worked the LEAST number of hours during the week is   6._____

   A. Brown   B. Green   C. Lane   D. Roe

7. The caretakers who did NOT work on Thursday are   7._____

   A. Doe, White, and Smith
   B. Green, Doe, and Lane
   C. Green, Doe, and Smith
   D. Green, Lane, and Smith

107

8. The day on which one caretaker worked ONLY 3 hours is   8.____
   A. Friday   B. Saturday   C. Thursday   D. Wednesday

9. The day on which ALL caretakers worked is   9.____
   A. Monday   B. Thursday   C. Tuesday   D. Wednesday

KEY (CORRECT ANSWERS)

1. A
2. B
3. C
4. B
5. B

6. B
7. B
8. C
9. C

TEST 4

Questions 1-6.

DIRECTIONS: Questions 1 through 6 are to be answered SOLELY on the basis of the table below which shows the initial requests made by staff for vacation. It is to be used with the RULES AND GUIDELINES to make the decisions and judgments called for in each of the questions.

\multicolumn{5}{c}{VACATION REQUESTS FOR THE ONE YEAR PERIOD FROM MAY 1, YEAR X THROUGH APRIL 30, YEAR Y}
Name	Work Assignment	Date Appointed	Accumulated Annual Leave Days	Vacation Periods Requested
DeMarco	MVO	Mar. 2003	25	May 3-21; Oct. 25-Nov. 5
Moore	Dispatcher	Dec. 1997	32	May 24-June 4; July 12-16
Kingston	MVO	Apr. 2007	28	May 24-June 11; Feb. 7-25
Green	MVO	June 2006	26	June 7-18; Sept. 6-24
Robinson	MVO	July 2008	30	June 28-July 9; Nov. 15-26
Reilly	MVO	Oct. 2009	23	July 5-9; Jan. 31-Mar. 3
Stevens	MVO	Sept. 1996	31	July 5-23; Oct. 4-29
Costello	MVO	Sept. 1998	31	July 5-30; Oct. 4-22
Maloney	Dispatcher	Aug. 1992	35	July 5-Aug. 6; Nov. 1-5
Hughes	Director	Feb. 1990	38	July 26-Sept. 3
Lord	MVO	Jan. 2010	20	Aug. 9-27; Feb. 7-25
Diaz	MVO	Dec. 2009	28	Aug. 9-Sept. 10
Krimsky	MVO	May 2006	22	Oct. 18-22: Nov. 22-Dec. 10

RULES AND GUIDELINES

1. The two Dispatchers cannot be on vacation at the same time, nor can a Dispatcher be on vacation at the same time as the Director.

2. For the period June 1 through September 30, not more than three MVO's can be on vacation at the same time.

3. For the period October 1 through May 31, not more than two MVO's at a time can be on vacation.

4. In cases where the same vacation time is requested by too many employees for all of them to be given the time under the rules, the requests of those who have worked the longest will be granted.

5. No employee may take more leave days than the number of annual leave days accumulated and shown in the table.

6. All vacation periods shown in the table and described in the questions below begin on a Monday and end on a Friday.

7. Employees work a five-day week (Monday through Friday). They are off weekends and holidays with no charges to leave balances. When a holiday falls on a Saturday or Sunday, employees are given the following Monday off without charge to annual leave.

2 (#4)

8. Holidays:
   May 31 October 25 January 1
   July 4 November 2 February 12
   September 6 November 25 February 21
   October 11 December 25 February 21

9. An employee shall be given any part of his initial requests that is permissible under the above rules and shall have first right to it despite any further adjustment of schedule.

---

1. Until adjustments in the vacation schedule can be made, the vacation dates that can be approved for Krimsky are

   A. Oct. 18-22; Nov. 22-Dec. 10
   B. Oct. 18-22; Nov. 29-Dec. 10
   C. Oct. 18-22 *only*
   D. Nov. 22-Dec. 10 *only*

1.____

2. Until adjustments in the vacation schedule can be made, the vacation dates that can be approved for Maloney are

   A. July 5-Aug. 6; Nov. 1-5
   B. July 5-23; Nov. 1-5
   C. July 5-9; Nov. 1-5
   D. Nov. 1-5 *only*

2.____

3. According to the table, Lord wants a vacation in August and another in February. Until adjustments in the vacation schedule can be made, he can be allowed to take _____ of the August vacation and _____ of the February vacation.

   A. all; none
   B. all; almost half
   C. almost all; almost half
   D. almost half; all

3.____

4. Costello cannot be given all the vacation he has requested because

   A. the MVO's who have more seniority than he has have requested time he wishes
   B. he does not have enough accumulated annual leave
   C. a dispatcher is applying for vacation at the same time as Costello
   D. there are five people who want vacation in July

4.____

5. According to the table, how many leave days will DeMarco be charged for his vacation from October 25 through November 5?

   A. 10   B. 9   C. 8   D. 7

5.____

6. How many leave days will Moore use if he uses the requested vacation allowable to him under the rules?

   A. 9   B. 10   C. 14   D. 15

6.____

KEY (CORRECT ANSWERS)

1. D
2. B
3. A
4. B
5. C
6. A

TEST 5

Questions 1-8.

DIRECTIONS: Questions 1 through 8 are to be answered SOLELY on the basis of Charts I, II, III, and IV. Assume that you are the supervisor of Operators R, S, T, U, V, W, and X, and it is your responsibility to schedule their lunch hours.

The charts each represent a possible scheduling of lunch hours during a lunch period from 11:30 - 2:00. An operator-hour is one hour of time spent by one operator. Each box on the chart represents one half-hour. The boxes marked L represent the time when each operator is scheduled to have her lunch hour. For example, in Chart I, next to Operator R, the boxes for 11:30 - 12:00 and 12:00 -12:30 are marked L. This means that Operator R is scheduled to have her lunch hour from 11:30 to 12:30.

I

	11:30-12:00	12:00-12:30	12:30-1:00	1:00-1:30	1:30-2:00
R	L	L			
S		L	L		
T		L	L		
U			L	L	
V			L	L	
W				L	L
X				L	L

II

	11:30-12:00	12:00-12:30	12:30-1:00	1:00-1:30	1:30-2:00
R				L	L
S		L	L		
T	L	L			
U			L	L	
V				L	L
W				L	L
X		L	L		

III

	11:30-12:00	12:00-12:30	12:30-1:00	1:00-1:30	1:30-2:00
R	L	L			
S				L	L
T	L	L			
U			L	L	
V	L	L			
W				L	L
X				L	L

IV

	11:30-12:00	12:00-12:30	12:30-1:00	1:00-1:30	1:30-2:00
R	L	L			
S	L	L			
T		L	L		
U			L	L	
V				L	L
W				L	L
X			L	L	

1. If, under the schedule represented in Chart II, Operator R has her lunch hour changed to 12:30-1:30, that leaves how many operator-hours of phone coverage from 1:00-2:00?   1.___

   A. 2   B. 2 1/2   C. 3   D. 4 1/2

2. If Operator S asks you whether she and Operator T may have the same lunch hour, you could accommodate her by using the schedule in Chart   2.___

   A. I   B. II   C. III   D. IV

3. From past experience you know that the part of the lunch period when the phones are busiest is from 12:30-1:30. Which chart shows the BEST phone coverage from 12:30 to 1:30?   3.___

   A. I   B. II   C. III   D. IV

4. At least three operators have the same lunch hour according to Chart(s)   4.___

   A. II and III   B. II and IV
   C. III only   D. IV only

5. Which chart would provide the POOREST phone coverage during the period 12:00-1:30, based on total number of operator-hours from 12:00 to 1:30? 5.____

   A. I   B. II   C. III   D. IV

6. Which chart would make it possible for U, W, and X to have the same lunch hour? 6.____

   A. I   B. II   C. III   D. IV

7. The portion of the lunch period during which the telephones are least busy is 11:30-12:30. 7.____
   Which chart is MOST likely to have been designed with that fact in mind?

   A. I   B. II   C. III   D. IV

8. Assume that you have decided to use Chart IV to schedule your operators' lunch hours on a specific day. Operator T asks you if she can have her lunch hour changed to 1:00-2:00. 8.____
   If you grant her request, how many operators will be working during the period 12:00 to 12:30?

   A. 1   B. 2   C. 4   D. 5

KEY (CORRECT ANSWERS)

1. D
2. A
3. B
4. A
5. A
6. C
7. C
8. D

TEST 6

Questions 1-13.

DIRECTIONS: Questions 1 through 13 consist of a statement. You are to indicate whether the statement is TRUE (T) or FALSE (F). *PRINT THE LETTER OF THE CORRECT ANSWER IN THE SPACE AT THE RIGHT.* Questions 1 through 13 are to be answered SOLELY on the basis of the information given in the table below.

\multicolumn{6}{c}{DEPARTMENT OF FERRIES ATTENDANTS WORK ASSIGNMENT - JULY 2003}
Name	Year Employed	Ferry Assigned	Hours of Work	Lunch Period	Days Off
Adams	1999	Hudson	7 AM - 3 PM	11-12	Fri. and Sat.
Baker	1992	Monroe	7 AM - 3 PM	11-12	Sun. and Mon.
Gunn	1995	Troy	8 AM - 4 PM	12-1	Fri. and Sat.
Hahn	1989	Erie	9 AM - 5 PM	1-2	Sat. and Sun.
King	1998	Albany	7 AM - 3 PM	11-12	Sun. and Mon.
Nash	1993	Hudson	11 AM - 7 PM	3-4	Sun. and Mon.
Olive	2003	Fulton	10 AM - 6 PM	2-3	Sat. and Sun.
Queen	2002	Albany	11 AM - 7 PM	3-4	Fri. and Sat.
Rose	1990	Troy	11 AM - 7 PM	3-4	Sun. and Mon.
Smith	1991	Monroe	10 AM - 6 PM	2-3	Fri. and Sat.

1. The chart shows that there are only five (5) ferries being used. 1.___

2. The attendant who has been working the LONGEST time is Rose. 2.___

3. The Troy has one more attendant assigned to it than the Erie. 3.___

4. Two (2) attendants are assigned to work from 10 P.M. to 6 A.M. 4.___

5. According to the chart, no more than one attendant was hired in any year. 5.___

6. The NEWEST employee is Olive. 6.___

7. There are as many attendants on the 7 to 3 shift as on the 11 to 7 shift. 7.___

8. MOST of the attendants have their lunch either between 12 and 1 or 2 and 3. 8.___

9. All the employees work four (4) hours before they go to lunch. 9.___

10. On the Hudson, Adams goes to lunch when Nash reports to work. 10.___

11. All the attendants who work on the 7 to 3 shift are off on Saturday and Sunday. 11.___

12. All the attendants have either a Saturday or Sunday as one of their days off. 12.___

13. At least two (2) attendants are assigned to each ferry. 13.___

KEY (CORRECT ANSWERS)

1.	F	6.	T	11.	F
2.	F	7.	T	12.	T
3.	T	8.	F	13.	F
4.	F	9.	T		
5.	T	10.	T		

PHILOSOPHY, PRINCIPLES, PRACTICES, AND TECHNICS
OF
SUPERVISION, ADMINISTRATION, MANAGEMENT, AND ORGANIZATION

TABLE OF CONTENTS

	Page
MEANING OF SUPERVISION	1
THE OLD AND THE NEW SUPERVISION	1
THE EIGHT (8) BASIC PRINCIPLES OF THE NEW SUPERVISION	1
I. Principle of Responsibility	1
II. Principle of Authority	2
III. Principle of Self-Growth	2
IV. Principle of Individual Worth	2
V. Principle of Creative Leadership	2
VI. Principle of Success and Failure	2
VII. Principle of Science	3
VIII. Principle of Cooperation	3
WHAT IS ADMINISTRATION?	3
I. Practices Commonly Classed as "Supervisory"	3
II. Practices Commonly Classed as "Administrative"	3
III. Practices Commonly Classed as Both "Supervisory" and "Administrative"	4
RESPONSIBILITIES OF THE SUPERVISOR	4
COMPETENCIES OF THE SUPERVISOR	4
THE PROFESSIONAL SUPERVISOR-EMPLOYEE RELATIONSHIP	4
MINI-TEXT IN SUPERVISION, ADMINISTRATION, MANAGEMENT, AND ORGANIZATION	5
I. Brief Highlights	5
A. Levels of Management	6
B. What the Supervisor Must Learn	6
C. A Definition of Supervision	6
D. Elements of the Team Concept	6
E. Principles of Organization	6
F. The Four Important Parts of Every Job	7
G. Principles of Delegation	7
H. Principles of Effective Communications	7
I. Principles of Work Improvement	7
J. Areas of Job Improvement	7
K. Seven Key Points in Making Improvements	8

	L.	Corrective Techniques for Job Improvement	8
	M.	A Planning Checklist	8
	N.	Five Characteristics of Good Directions	9
	O.	Types of Directions	9
	P.	Controls	9
	Q.	Orienting the New Employee	9
	R.	Checklist for Orienting New Employees	9
	S.	Principles of Learning	10
	T.	Causes of Poor Performance	10
	U.	Four Major Steps in On-the-Job Instructions	10
	V.	Employees Want Five Things	10
	W.	Some Don'ts in Regard to Praise	11
	X.	How to Gain Your Workers' Confidence	11
	Y.	Sources of Employee Problems	11
	Z.	The Supervisor's Key to Discipline	11
	AA.	Five Important Processes of Management	12
	BB.	When the Supervisor Fails to Plan	12
	CC.	Fourteen General Principles of Management	12
	DD.	Change	12
II.	Brief Topical Summaries		13
	A.	Who/What is the Supervisor?	13
	B.	The Sociology of Work	13
	C.	Principles and Practices of Supervision	14
	D.	Dynamic Leadership	14
	E.	Processes for Solving Problems	15
	F.	Training for Results	15
	G.	Health, Safety, and Accident Prevention	16
	H.	Equal Employment Opportunity	16
	I.	Improving Communications	16
	J.	Self-Development	17
	K.	Teaching and Training	17
		1. The Teaching Process	17
		a. Preparation	17
		b. Presentation	18
		c. Summary	18
		d. Application	18
		e. Evaluation	18
		2. Teaching Methods	18
		a. Lecture	18
		b. Discussion	18
		c. Demonstration	19
		d. Performance	19
		e. Which Method to Use	19

PHILOSOPHY, PRINCIPLES, PRACTICES, AND TECHNICS
OF
SUPERVISION, ADMINISTRATION, MANAGEMENT, AND ORGANIZATION

MEANING OF SUPERVISION

The extension of the democratic philosophy has been accompanied by an extension in the scope of supervision. Modern leaders and supervisors no longer think of supervision in the narrow sense of being confined chiefly to visiting employees, supplying materials, or rating the staff. They regard supervision as being intimately related to all the concerned agencies of society, they speak of the supervisor's function in terms of "growth," rather than the "improvement" of employees.

This modern concept of supervision may be defined as follows: Supervision is leadership and the development of leadership within groups which are cooperatively engaged in inspection, research, training, guidance, and evaluation.

THE OLD AND THE NEW SUPERVISION

TRADITIONAL
1. Inspection
2. Focused on the employee
3. Visitation
4. Random and haphazard
5. Imposed and authoritarian
6. One person usually

MODERN
1. Study and analysis
2. Focused on aims, materials, methods, supervisors, employees, environment
3. Demonstrations, intervisitation, workshops, directed reading, bulletins, etc.
4. Definitely organized and planned (scientific)
5. Cooperative and democratic
6. Many persons involved (creative)

THE EIGHT (8) BASIC PRINCIPLES OF THE NEW SUPERVISION

I. Principle of Responsibility
Authority to act and responsibility for acting must be joined.
   A. If you give responsibility, give authority.
   B. Define employee duties clearly.
   C. Protect employees from criticism by others.
   D. Recognize the rights as well as obligations of employees.
   E. Achieve the aims of a democratic society insofar as it is possible within the area of your work.
   F. Establish a situation favorable to training and learning.
   G. Accept ultimate responsibility for everything done in your section, unit, office, division, department.
   H. Good administration and good supervision are inseparable.

II. Principle of Authority
   The success of the supervisor is measured by the extent to which the power of authority is not used.
   A. Exercise simplicity and informality in supervision
   B. Use the simplest machinery of supervision
   C. If it is good for the organization as a whole, it is probably justified.
   D. Seldom be arbitrary or authoritative.
   E. Do not base your work on the power of position or of personality.
   F. Permit and encourage the free expression of opinions.

III. Principle of Self-Growth
   The success of the supervisor is measured by the extent to which, and the speed with which, he is no longer needed.
   A. Base criticism on principles, not on specifics.
   B. Point out higher activities to employees.
   C. Train for self-thinking by employees to meet new situations.
   D. Stimulate initiative, self-reliance, and individual responsibility
   E. Concentrate on stimulating the growth of employees rather than on removing defects.

IV. Principle of Individual Worth
   Respect for the individual is a paramount consideration in supervision.
   A. Be human and sympathetic in dealing with employees.
   B. Don't nag about things to be done.
   C. Recognize the individual differences among employees and seek opportunities to permit best expression of each personality.

V. Principle of Creative Leadership
   The best supervision is that which is not apparent to the employee.
   A. Stimulate, don't drive employees to creative action.
   B. Emphasize doing good things.
   C. Encourage employees to do what they do best.
   D. Do not be too greatly concerned with details of subject or method.
   E. Do not be concerned exclusively with immediate problems and activities.
   F. Reveal higher activities and make them both desired and maximally possible.
   G. Determine procedures in the light of each situation but see that these are derived from a sound basic philosophy.
   H. Aid, inspire, and lead so as to liberate the creative spirit latent in all good employees.

VI. Principle of Success and Failure
   There are no unsuccessful employees, only unsuccessful supervisors who have failed to give proper leadership.
   A. Adapt suggestions to the capacities, attitudes, and prejudices of employees.
   B. Be gradual, be progressive, be persistent.
   C. Help the employee find the general principle; have the employee apply his own problem to the general principle.
   D. Give adequate appreciation for good work and honest effort.
   E. Anticipate employee difficulties and help to prevent them.
   F. Encourage employees to do the desirable things they will do anyway.
   G. Judge your supervision by the results it secures.

VII. Principle of Science
Successful supervision is scientific, objective, and experimental. It is based on facts, not on prejudices.
   A. Be cumulative in results.
   B. Never divorce your suggestions from the goals of training.
   C. Don't be impatient of results.
   D. Keep all matters on a professional, not a personal, level.
   E. Do not be concerned exclusively with immediate problems and activities.
   F. Use objective means of determining achievement and rating where possible.

VIII. Principle of Cooperation
Supervision is a cooperative enterprise between supervisor and employee.
   A. Begin with conditions as they are.
   B. Ask opinions of all involved when formulating policies.
   C. Organization is as good as its weakest link.
   D. Let employees help to determine policies and department programs.
   E. Be approachable and accessible—physically and mentally.
   F. Develop pleasant social relationships.

WHAT IS ADMINISTRATION

Administration is concerned with providing the environment, the material facilities, and the operational procedures that will promote the maximum growth and development of supervisors and employees. (Organization is an aspect and a concomitant of administration.)

There is no sharp line of demarcation between supervision and administration; these functions are intimately interrelated and, often, overlapping. They are complementary activities.

I. Practices Commonly Classed as "Supervisory"
   A. Conducting employees' conferences
   B. Visiting sections, units, offices, divisions, departments
   C. Arranging for demonstrations
   D. Examining plans
   E. Suggesting professional reading
   F. Interpreting bulletins
   G. Recommending in-service training courses
   H. Encouraging experimentation
   I. Appraising employee morale
   J. Providing for intervisitation

II. Practices Commonly Classified as "Administrative"
   A. Management of the office
   B. Arrangement of schedules for extra duties
   C. Assignment of rooms or areas
   D. Distribution of supplies
   E. Keeping records and reports
   F. Care of audio-visual materials
   G. Keeping inventory records
   H. Checking record cards and books

I. Programming special activities
J. Checking on the attendance and punctuality of employees

III. Practices Commonly Classified as Both "Supervisory" and "Administrative"
   A. Program construction
   B. Testing or evaluating outcomes
   C. Personnel accounting
   D. Ordering instructional materials

RESPONSIBILITIES OF THE SUPERVISOR

A person employed in a supervisory capacity must constantly be able to improve his own efficiency and ability. He represent the employer to the employees and only continuous self-examination can make him a capable supervisor.

Leadership and training are the supervisor's responsibility. An efficient working unit is one in which the employees work with the supervisor. It is his job to bring out the best in his employees. He must always be relaxed, courteous, and calm in his association with his employees. Their feelings are important, and a harsh attitude does not develop the most efficient employees.

COMPETENCES OF THE SUPERVISOR

I. Complete knowledge of the duties and responsibilities of his position.
II. To be able to organize a job, plan ahead, and carry through.
III. To have self-confidence and initiative.
IV. To be able to handle the unexpected situation and make quick decisions.
V. To be able to properly train subordinates in the positions they are best suited for.
VI. To be able to keep good human relations among his subordinates.
VII. To be able to keep good human relations between his subordinates and himself and to earn their respect and trust.

THE PROFESSIONAL SUPERVISOR-EMPLOYEE RELATIONSHIP

There are two kinds of efficiency: one kind is only apparent and is produced in organizations through the exercise of mere discipline; this is but a simulation of the second, or true, efficiency which springs from spontaneous cooperation. If you are a manager, no matter how great or small your responsibility, it is your job, in the final analysis, to create and develop this involuntary cooperation among the people whom you supervise. For, no matter how powerful a combination of money, machines, and materials a company may have, this is a dead and sterile thing without a team of willing, thinking, and articulate people to guide it.

The following 21 points are presented as indicative of the exemplary basic relationship that should exist between supervisor and employee:

1. Each person wants to be liked and respected by his fellow employee and wants to be treated with consideration and respect by his superior.
2. The most competent employee will make an error. However, in a unit where good relations exist between the supervisor and his employees, tenseness and fear do not exist. Thus, errors are not hidden or covered up, and the efficiency of a unit is not impaired.

3. Subordinates resent rules, regulations, or orders that are unreasonable or unexplained.
4. Subordinates are quick to resent unfairness, harshness, injustices, and favoritism.
5. An employee will accept responsibility if he knows that he will be complimented for a job well done, and not too harshly chastised for failure; that his supervisor will check the cause of the failure, and, if it was the supervisor's fault, he will assume the blame therefore. If it was the employee's fault, his supervisor will explain the correct method or means of handling the responsibility.
6. An employee wants to receive credit for a suggestion he has made, that is used. If a suggestion cannot be used, the employee is entitled to an explanation. The supervisor should not say "no" and close the subject.
7. Fear and worry slow up a worker's ability. Poor working environment can impair his physical and mental health. A good supervisor avoids forceful methods, threats, and arguments to get a job done.
8. A forceful supervisor is able to train his employees individually and as a team, and is able to motivate them in the proper channels.
9. A mature supervisor is able to properly evaluate his subordinates and to keep them happy and satisfied.
10. A sensitive supervisor will never patronize his subordinates.
11. A worthy supervisor will respect his employees' confidences.
12. Definite and clear-cut responsibilities should be assigned to each executive.
13. Responsibility should always be coupled with corresponding authority.
14. No change should be made in the scope or responsibilities of a position without a definite understanding to that effect on the part of all persons concerned.
15. No executive or employee, occupying a single position in the organization, should be subject to definite orders from more than one source.
16. Orders should never be given to subordinates over the head of a responsible executive. Rather than do this, the officer in question should be supplanted.
17. Criticisms of subordinates should, whoever possible, be made privately, and in no case should a subordinate be criticized in the presence of executives or employees of equal or lower rank.
18. No dispute or difference between executives or employees as to authority or responsibilities should be considered too trivial for prompt and careful adjudication.
19. Promotions, wage changes, and disciplinary action should always be approved by the executive immediately superior to the one directly responsible.
20. No executive or employee should ever be required, or expected, to be at the same time an assistant to, and critic of, another.
21. Any executive whose work is subject to regular inspection should, wherever practicable, be given the assistance and facilities necessary to enable him to maintain an independent check of the quality of his work.

MINI-TEXT IN SUPERVISION, ADMINISTRATION, MANAGEMENT, AND ORGANIZATION

I. Brief Highlights

Listed concisely and sequentially are major headings and important data in the field for quick recall and review.

A. Levels of Management
Any organization of some size has several levels of management. In terms of a ladder, the levels are:

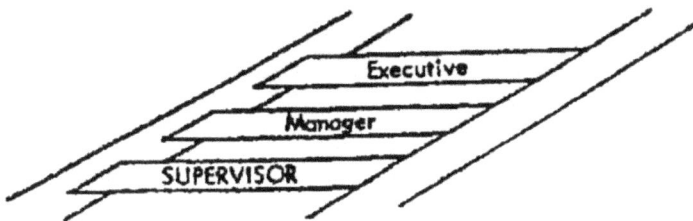

The first level is very important because it is the beginning point of management leadership.

B. What the Supervisor Must Learn
A supervisor must learn to:
1. Deal with people and their differences
2. Get the job done through people
3. Recognize the problems when they exist
4. Overcome obstacles to good performance
5. Evaluate the performance of people
6. Check his own performance in terms of accomplishment

C. A Definition of Supervisor
The term supervisor means any individual having authority, in the interests of the employer, to hire, transfer, suspend, lay-off, recall, promote, discharge, assign, reward, or discipline other employees or responsibility to direct them, or to adjust their grievances, or effectively to recommend such action, if, in connection with the foregoing, exercise of such authority is not of a merely routine or clerical nature but requires the use of independent judgment.

D. Elements of the Team Concept
What is involved in teamwork? The component parts are:
1. Members
2. A leader
3. Goals
4. Plans
5. Cooperation
6. Spirit

E. Principles of Organization
1. A team member must know what his job is.
2. Be sure that the nature and scope of a job are understood.
3. Authority and responsibility should be carefully spelled out.
4. A supervisor should be permitted to make the maximum number of decisions affecting his employees.
5. Employees should report to only one supervisor.
6. A supervisor should direct only as many employees as he can handle effectively.
7. An organization plan should be flexible.

8. Inspection and performance of work should be separate.
9. Organizational problems should receive immediate attention.
10. Assign work in line with ability and experience.

F. The Four Important Parts of Every Job
1. Inherent in every job is the *accountability* for results.
2. A second set of factors in every job is *responsibilities*.
3. Along with duties and responsibilities one must have the *authority* to act within certain limits without obtaining permission to proceed.
4. No job exists in a vacuum. The supervisor is surrounded by key *relationships*.

G. Principles of Delegation
Where work is delegated for the first time, the supervisor should think in terms of these questions:
1. Who is best qualified to do this?
2. Can an employee improve his abilities by doing this?
3. How long should an employee spend on this?
4. Are there any special problems for which he will need guidance?
5. How broad a delegation can I make?

H. Principles of Effective Communications
1. Determine the media.
2. To whom directed?
3. Identification and source authority.
4. Is communication understood?

I. Principles of Work Improvement
1. Most people usually do only the work which is assigned to them.
2. Workers are likely to fit assigned work into the time available to perform it.
3. A good workload usually stimulates output.
4. People usually do their best work when they know that results will be reviewed or inspected.
5. Employees usually feel that someone else is responsible for conditions of work, workplace layout, job methods, type of tools/equipment, and other such factors.
6. Employees are usually defensive about their job security.
7. Employees have natural resistance to change.
8. Employees can support or destroy a supervisor.
9. A supervisor usually earns the respect of his people through his personal example of diligence and efficiency.

J. Areas of Job Improvement
The areas of job improvement are quite numerous, but the most common ones which a supervisor can identify and utilize are:
1. Departmental layout
2. Flow of work
3. Workplace layout
4. Utilization of manpower
5. Work methods
6. Materials handling

7. Utilization
8. Motion economy

K. Seven Key Points in Making Improvements
1. Select the job to be improved
2. Study how it is being done now
3. Question the present method
4. Determine actions to be taken
5. Chart proposed method
6. Get approval and apply
7. Solicit worker participation

I. Corrective Techniques of Job Improvement
Specific Problems
1. Size of workload
2. Inability to meet schedules
3. Strain and fatigue
4. Improper use of men and skills
5. Waste, poor quality, unsafe conditions
6. Bottleneck conditions that hinder output
7. Poor utilization of equipment and machine
8. Efficiency and productivity of labor

General Improvement
1. Departmental layout
2. Flow of work
3. Work plan layout
4. Utilization of manpower
5. Work methods
6. Materials handling
7. Utilization of equipment
8. Motion economy

Corrective Techniques
1. Study with scale model
2. Flow chart study
3. Motion analysis
4. Comparison of units produced to standard allowance
5. Methods analysis
6. Flow chart and equipment study
7. Down time vs. running time
8. Motion analysis

M. A Planning Checklist
1. Objectives
2. Controls
3. Delegations
4. Communications
5. Resources
6. Manpower

7. Equipment
8. Supplies and materials
9. Utilization of time
10. Safety
11. Money
12. Work
13. Timing of improvements

N. Five Characteristics of Good Directions
In order to get results, directions must be:
1. Possible of accomplishment
2. Agreeable with worker interests
3. Related to mission
4. Planned and complete
5. Unmistakably clear

O. Types of Directions
1. Demands or direct orders
2. Requests
3. Suggestion or implication
4. volunteering

P. Controls
A typical listing of the overall areas in which the supervisor should establish controls might be:
1. Manpower
2. Materials
3. Quality of work
4. Quantity of work
5. Time
6. Space
7. Money
8. Methods

Q. Orienting the New Employee
1. Prepare for him
2. Welcome the new employee
3. Orientation for the job
4. Follow-up

R. Checklist for Orienting New Employees   Yes   No
1. Do you appreciate the feelings of new employees when they first report for work?   ___   ___
2. Are you aware of the fact that the new employee must make a big adjustment to his job?   ___   ___
3. Have you given him good reasons for liking the job and the organization?   ___   ___
4. Have you prepared for his first day on the job?   ___   ___
5. Did you welcome him cordially and make him feel needed?   ___   ___

	Yes	No

6. Did you establish rapport with him so that he feels free to talk and discuss matters with you? ___ ___
7. Did you explain his job to him and his relationship to you? ___ ___
8. Does he know that his work will be evaluated periodically on a basis that is fair and objective? ___ ___
9. Did you introduce him to his fellow workers in such a way that they are likely to accept him? ___ ___
10. Does he know what employee benefits he will receive? ___ ___
11. Does he understand the importance of being on the job and what to do if he must leave his duty station? ___ ___
12. Has he been impressed with the importance of accident prevention and safe practice? ___ ___
13. Does he generally know his way around the department? ___ ___
14. Is he under the guidance of a sponsor who will teach the right way of doing things? ___ ___
15. Do you plan to follow-up so that he will continue to adjust successfully to his job? ___ ___

S. Principles of Learning
  1. Motivation
  2. Demonstration or explanation
  3. Practice

T. Causes of Poor Performance
  1. Improper training for job
  2. Wrong tools
  3. Inadequate directions
  4. Lack of supervisory follow-up
  5. Poor communications
  6. Lack of standards of performance
  7. Wrong work habits
  8. Low morale
  9. Other

U. Four Major Steps in On-The-Job Instruction
  1. Prepare the worker
  2. Present the operation
  3. Tryout performance
  4. Follow-up

V. Employees Want Five Things
  1. Security
  2. Opportunity
  3. Recognition
  4. Inclusion
  5. Expression

W. Some Don'ts in Regard to Praise
1. Don't praise a person for something he hasn't done.
2. Don't praise a person unless you can be sincere.
3. Don't be sparing in praise just because your superior withholds it from you.
4. Don't let too much time elapse between good performance and recognition of it

X. How to Gain Your Workers' Confidence
Methods of developing confidence include such things as:
1. Knowing the interests, habits, hobbies of employees
2. Admitting your own inadequacies
3. Sharing and telling of confidence in others
4. Supporting people when they are in trouble
5. Delegating matters that can be well handled
6. Being frank and straightforward about problems and working conditions
7. Encouraging others to bring their problems to you
8. Taking action on problems which impede worker progress

Y. Sources of Employee Problems
On-the-job causes might be such things as:
1. A feeling that favoritism is exercised in assignments
2. Assignment of overtime
3. An undue amount of supervision
4. Changing methods or systems
5. Stealing of ideas or trade secrets
6. Lack of interest in job
7. Threat of reduction in force
8. Ignorance or lack of communications
9. Poor equipment
10. Lack of knowing how supervisor feels toward employee
11. Shift assignments

Off-the-job problems might have to do with:
1. Health
2. Finances
3. Housing
4. Family

Z. The Supervisor's Key to Discipline
There are several key points about discipline which the supervisor should keep in mind:
1. Job discipline is one of the disciplines of life and is directed by the supervisor.
2. It is more important to correct an employee fault than to fix blame for it.
3. Employee performance is affected by problems both on the job and off.
4. Sudden or abrupt changes in behavior can be indications of important employee problems.
5. Problems should be dealt with as soon as possible after they are identified.
6. The attitude of the supervisor may have more to do with solving problems than the techniques of problem solving.
7. Correction of employee behavior should be resorted to only after the supervisor is sure that training or counseling will not be helpful.

8. Be sure to document your disciplinary actions.
9. Make sure that you are disciplining on the basis of facts rather than personal feelings.
10. Take each disciplinary step in order, being careful not to make snap judgments, or decisions based on impatience.

AA. Five Important Processes of Management
1. Planning
2. Organizing
3. Scheduling
4. Controlling
5. Motivating

BB. When the Supervisor Fails to Plan
1. Supervisor creates impression of not knowing his job
2. May lead to excessive overtime
3. Job runs itself—supervisor lacks control
4. Deadlines and appointments missed
5. Parts of the work go undone
6. Work interrupted by emergencies
7. Sets a bad example
8. Uneven workload creates peaks and valleys
9. Too much time on minor details at expense of more important tasks

CC. Fourteen General Principles of Management
1. Division of work
2. Authority and responsibility
3. Discipline
4. Unity of command
5. Unity of direction
6. Subordination of individual interest to general interest
7. Remuneration of personnel
8. Centralization
9. Scalar chain
10. Order
11. Equity
12. Stability of tenure of personnel
13. Initiative
14. Esprit de corps

DD. Change

Bringing about change is perhaps attempted more often, and yet less well understood, than anything else the supervisor does. How do people generally react to change? (People tend to resist change that is imposed upon them by other individuals or circumstances.

Change is characteristic of every situation. It is a part of every real endeavor where the efforts of people are concerned.

1. Why do people resist change?
   People may resist change because of:
   a. Fear of the unknown
   b. Implied criticism
   c. Unpleasant experiences in the past
   d. Fear of loss of status
   e. Threat to the ego
   f. Fear of loss of economic stability

2. How can we best overcome the resistance to change?
   In initiating change, take these steps:
   a. Get ready to sell
   b. Identify sources of help
   c. Anticipate objections
   d. Sell benefits
   e. Listen in depth
   f. Follow up

II. Brief Topical Summaries

   A. Who/What is the Supervisor?
      1. The supervisor is often called the "highest level employee and the lowest level manager."
      2. A supervisor is a member of both management and the work group. He acts as a bridge between the two.
      3. Most problems in supervision are in the area of human relations, or people problems.
      4. Employees expect: Respect, opportunity to learn and to advance, and a sense of belonging, and so forth.
      5. Supervisors are responsible for directing people and organizing work. Planning is of paramount importance.
      6. A position description is a set of duties and responsibilities inherent to a given position.
      7. It is important to keep the position description up-to-date and to provide each employee with his own copy.

   B. The Sociology of Work
      1. People are alike in many ways; however, each individual is unique.
      2. The supervisor is challenged in getting to know employee differences. Acquiring skills in evaluating individuals is an asset.
      3. Maintaining meaningful working relationships in the organization is of great importance.
      4. The supervisor has an obligation to help individuals to develop to their fullest potential.
      5. Job rotation on a planned basis helps to build versatility and to maintain interest and enthusiasm in work groups.
      6. Cross training (job rotation) provides backup skills.

7. The supervisor can help reduce tension by maintaining a sense of humor, providing guidance to employees, and by making reasonable and timely decisions. Employees respond favorably to working under reasonably predictable circumstances.
8. Change is characteristic of all managerial behavior. The supervisor must adjust to changes in procedures, new methods, technological changes, and to a number of new and sometimes challenging situations.
9. To overcome the natural tendency for people to resist change, the supervisor should become more skillful in initiating change.

C. Principles and Practices of Supervision
1. Employees should be required to answer to only one superior.
2. A supervisor can effectively direct only a limited number of employees, depending upon the complexity, variety, and proximity of the jobs involved.
3. The organizational chart presents the organization in graphic form. It reflects lines of authority and responsibility as well as interrelationships of units within the organization.
4. Distribution of work can be improved through an analysis using the "Work Distribution Chart."
5. The "Work Distribution Chart" reflects the division of work within a unit in understandable form.
6. When related tasks are given to an employee, he has a better chance of increasing his skills through training.
7. The individual who is given the responsibility for tasks must also be given the appropriate authority to insure adequate results.
8. The supervisor should delegate repetitive, routine work. Preparation of recurring reports, maintaining leave and attendance records are some examples.
9. Good discipline is essential to good task performance. Discipline is reflected in the actions of employees on the job in the absence of supervision.
10. Disciplinary action may have to be taken when the positive aspects of discipline have failed. Reprimand, warning, and suspension are examples of disciplinary action.
11. If a situation calls for a reprimand, be sure it is deserved and remember it is to be done in private.

D. Dynamic Leadership
1. A style is a personal method or manner of exerting influence.
2. Authoritarian leaders often see themselves as the source of power and authority.
3. The democratic leader often perceives the group as the source of authority and power.
4. Supervisors tend to do better when using the pattern of leadership that is most natural for them.
5. Social scientists suggest that the effective supervisor use the leadership style that best fits the problem or circumstances involved.
6. All four styles—telling, selling, consulting, joining—have their place. Using one does not preclude using the other at another time.

7. The theory X point of view assumes that the average person dislikes work, will avoid it whenever possible, and must be coerced to achieve organizational objectives.
8. The theory Y point of view assumes that the average person considers work to be a natural as play, and, when the individual is committed, he requires little supervision or direction to accomplish desired objectives.
9. The leader's basic assumptions concerning human behavior and human nature affect his actions, decisions, and other managerial practices.
10. Dissatisfaction among employees is often present, but difficult to isolate. The supervisor should seek to weaken dissatisfaction by keeping promises, being sincere and considerate, keeping employees informed, and so forth.
11. Constructive suggestions should be encouraged during the natural progress of the work.

E. Processes for Solving Problems
1. People find their daily tasks more meaningful and satisfying when they can improve them.
2. The causes of problems, or the key factors, are often hidden in the background. Ability to solve problems often involves the ability to isolate them from their backgrounds. There is some substance to the cliché that some persons "can't see the forest for the trees."
3. New procedures are often developed from old ones. Problems should be broken down into manageable parts. New ideas can be adapted from old one.
4. People think differently in problem-solving situations. Using a logical, patterned approach is often useful. One approach found to be useful includes these steps:
   a. Define the problem
   b. Establish objectives
   c. Get the facts
   d. Weigh and decide
   e. Take action
   f. Evaluate action

F. Training for Results
1. Participants respond best when they feel training is important to them.
2. The supervisor has responsibility for the training and development of those who report to him.
3. When training is delegated to others, great care must be exercised to insure the trainer has knowledge, aptitude, and interest for his work as a trainer.
4. Training (learning) of some type goes on continually. The most successful supervisor makes certain the learning contributes in a productive manner to operational goals.
5. New employees are particularly susceptible to training. Older employees facing new job situations require specific training, as well as having need for development and growth opportunities.
6. Training needs require continuous monitoring.
7. The training officer of an agency is a professional with a responsibility to assist supervisors in solving training problems.

8. Many of the self-development steps important to the supervisor's own growth are equally important to the development of peers and subordinates. Knowledge of these is important when the supervisor consults with others on development and growth opportunities.

G. Health, Safety, and Accident Prevention
1. Management-minded supervisors take appropriate measures to assist employees in maintaining health and in assuring safe practices in the work environment.
2. Effective safety training and practices help to avoid injury and accidents.
3. Safety should be a management goal. All infractions of safety which are observed should be corrected without exception.
4. Employees' safety attitude, training and instruction, provision of safe tools and equipment, supervision, and leadership are considered highly important factors which contribute to safety and which can be influenced directly by supervisors.
5. When accidents do occur, they should be investigated promptly for very important reasons, including the fact that information which is gained can be used to prevent accidents in the future.

H. Equal Employment Opportunity
1. The supervisor should endeavor to treat all employees fairly, without regard to religion, race, sex, or national origin.
2. Groups tend to reflect the attitude of the leader. Prejudice can be detected even in very subtle form. Supervisors must strive to create a feeling of mutual respect and confidence in every employee.
3. Complete utilization of all human resources is a national goal. Equitable consideration should be accorded women in the work force, minority-group members, the physically and mentally handicapped, and the older employee. The important question is: "Who can do the job?"
4. Training opportunities, recognition for performance, overtime assignments, promotional opportunities, and all other personnel actions are to be handled on an equitable basis.

I. Improving Communications
1. Communications is achieving understanding between the sender and the receiver of a message. It also means sharing information—the creation of understanding.
2. Communication is basic to all human activity. Words are means of conveying meanings; however, real meanings are in people.
3. There are very practical differences in the effectiveness of one-way, impersonal, and two-way communications. Words spoken face-to-face are better understood. Telephone conversations are effective, but lack the rapport of person-to-person exchanges. The whole person communicates.
4. Cooperation and communication in an organization go hand in hand. When there is a mutual respect between people, spelling out rules and procedures for communicating is unnecessary.
5. There are several barriers to effective communications. These include failure to listen with respect and understanding, lack of skill in feedback, and misinterpreting the meanings of words used by the speaker. It is also common

practice to listen to what we want to hear, and tune out things we do not want to hear.
6. Communication is management's chief problem. The supervisor should accept the challenge to communicate more effectively and to improve interagency and intra-agency communications.
7. The supervisor may often plan for and conduct meetings. The planning phase is critical and may determine the success or the failure of a meeting.
8. Speaking before groups usually requires extra effort. Stage fright may never disappear completely, but it can be controlled.

J. Self-Development
1. Every employee is responsible for his own self-development.
2. Toastmaster and toastmistress clubs offer opportunities to improve skills in oral communications.
3. Planning for one's own self-development is of vital importance. Supervisors know their own strengths and limitations better than anyone else.
4. Many opportunities are open to aid the supervisor in his developmental efforts, including job assignments; training opportunities, both governmental and non-governmental—to include universities and professional conferences and seminars.
5. Programmed instruction offers a means of studying at one's own rate.
6. Where difficulties may arise from a supervisor's being away from his work for training, he may participate in televised home study or correspondence courses to meet his self-development needs.

K. Teaching and Training
1. The Teaching Process
Teaching is encouraging and guiding the learning activities of students toward established goals. In most cases this process consists of five steps: preparation, presentation, summarization, evaluation, and application.

   a. Preparation
   Preparation is two-fold in nature; that of the supervisor and the employee. Preparation by the supervisor is absolutely essential to success. He must know what, when, where, how, and whom he will teach. Some of the factors that should be considered are:
   1) The objectives
   2) The materials needed
   3) The methods to be used
   4) Employee participation
   5) Employee interest
   6) Training aids
   7) Evaluation
   8) Summarization

   Employee preparation consists in preparing the employee to receive the material. Probably the most important single factor in the preparation of the employee is arousing and maintaining his interest. He must know the objectives of the training, why he is there, how the material can be used, and its importance to him.

b. Presentation
In presentation, have a carefully designed plan and follow it. The plan should be accurate and complete, yet flexible enough to meet situations as they arise. The method of presentation will be determined by the particular situation and objectives.

c. Summary
A summary should be made at the end of every training unit and program. In addition, there may be internal summaries depending on the nature of the material being taught. The important thing is that the trainee must always be able to understand how each part of the new material relates to the whole.

d. Application
The supervisor must arrange work so the employee will be given a chance to apply new knowledge or skills while the material is still clear in his mind and interest is high. The trainee does not really know whether he has learned the material until he has been given a chance to apply it. If the material is not applied, it loses most of its value.

e. Evaluation
The purpose of all training is to promote learning. To determine whether the training has been a success or failure, the supervisor must evaluate this learning.
In the broadest sense, evaluation includes all the devices, methods, skills, and techniques used by the supervisor to keep himself and the employees informed as to their progress toward the objectives they are pursuing. The extent to which the employee has mastered the knowledge, skills, and abilities, or changed his attitudes, as determined by the program objectives, is the extent to which instruction has succeeded or failed.
Evaluation should not be confined to the end of the lesson, day, or program but should be used continuously. We shall note later the way this relates to the rest of the teaching process.

2. Teaching Methods
A teaching method is a pattern of identifiable student and instructor activity used in presenting training material.
All supervisors are faced with the problem of deciding which method should be used at a given time.

a. Lecture
The lecture is direct oral presentation of material by the supervisor. The present trend is to place less emphasis on the trainer's activity and more on that of the trainee.

b. Discussion
Teaching by discussion or conference involves using questions and other techniques to arouse interest and focus attention upon certain areas, and by doing so creating a learning situation. This can be one of the most

valuable methods because it gives the employees an opportunity to express their ideas and pool their knowledge.

    c. Demonstration
The demonstration is used to teach how something works or how to do something. It can be used to show a principle or what the results of a series of actions will be. A well-staged demonstration is particularly effective because it shows proper methods of performance in a realistic manner.

    d. Performance
Performance is one of the most fundamental of all learning techniques or teaching methods. The trainee may be able to tell how a specific operation should be performed but he cannot be sure he knows how to perform the operation until he has done so.
As with all methods, there are certain advantages and disadvantages to each method.

    e. Which Method to Use
Moreover, there are other methods and techniques of teaching. It is difficult to use any method without other methods entering into it. In any learning situation, a combination of methods is usually more effective than any one method alone.

Finally, evaluation must be integrated into the other aspects of the teaching-learning process.

It must be used in the motivation of the trainees; it must be used to assist in developing understanding during the training; and it must be related to employee application of the results of training.

This is distinctly the role of the supervisor.

www.ingramcontent.com/pod-product-compliance
Lightning Source LLC
Chambersburg PA
CBHW081824300426
44116CB00014B/2480